"Paul Schullery is a master of the essayist's and memoirist's craft. His prose is clean and cogent, witty and wise. He pays great attention. He has been out among the bears—often with the biologists who study them—and this has given him a fine understanding of and appreciation for these formidable mammals. *The Bear Doesn't Know* is educating and entertaining, a thoroughly delightful paean to these very special creatures with whom we are privileged to share the earth."
—Charles Fergus, author of the Gideon Stoltz Mystery series

"From John Muir forward, writers in the American West have been trying to make sense of wild creatures and places. Paul Schullery, with his always lyrical, thoughtful, and, at times, witty prose, has been one of the best modern observers, having close association with this nation's most venerable natural destination, Yellowstone. No animals are more synonymous with Yellowstone than bears. Schullery takes us into Yellowstone and farther afield. In *The Bear Doesn't Know*, Schullery, much to our delight, comes out of his own thankfully-brief hibernation and regales us with inspiring bear stories. He introduces us to the real bruin, even better than myth, and, along the way, tugs on our heartstrings to have us care more about their survival in this briskly paced world. He bestows bruins with the respect they deserve and reminds us that the responsibility of coexistence is on us. *The Bear Doesn't Know* is a wonderful read that stays with you long after you turn the last page."
—Todd Wilkinson, coauthor of *Grizzlies of Pilgrim Creek: An Intimate Portrait of 399, The Most Famous Bear of Greater Yellowstone*

T0338842

The Bear Doesn't Know

Life and Wonder in Bear Country

PAUL SCHULLERY

University of Nebraska Press

LINCOLN

Library of Congress Cataloging-in-Publication Data
Names: Schullery, Paul, author.
Title: The bear doesn't know: life and wonder in bear
country / Paul Schullery.
Description: Lincoln: University of Nebraska Press, [2021] |
Includes bibliographical references.
Identifiers: LCCN 2021007062
ISBN 9781496226068 (paperback)
ISBN 9781496229328 (epub)
ISBN 9781496229335 (pdf)
Subjects: LCSH: Schullery, Paul. | Park naturalists—United
States—Biography. | Bears—Yellowstone National Park. |
Bears—Alaska—Denali National Park and Preserve. |
Wildlife management—Yellowstone National Park—
History. | Wildlife management—Alaska—Denali
National Park and Preserve—History.
Classification: LCC QL737.C27 S355 2021 |
DDC 599.7809787/52—dc23
LC record available at https://lccn.loc.gov/2021007062

Set in Minion Pro by Mikala R. Kolander.

For Linda Wiggins and Steve Herrero

Like the grizzly following his nose through life from one interesting smell to another, I too have wandered foot-loose and fancy-free, my feet pointed only by curiosity to see what lay over the next hill and mountain ridge.

ANDY RUSSELL

If any animal in the forest could benefit from a clearer understanding by humankind, it is the bear.

TERRY DEBRUYN

Everybody's got a bear story to tell.

SUSAN SNYDER

CONTENTS

Part 4. The Literary Bear

ILLUSTRATIONS

Bear Stories and the Art of the Memoir

We ask much of bears—entertainment, beauty, sport, and adventure certainly, but also inspiration, mystery, magic, and, if we're really paying attention, wisdom. And patience; I will never understand why they are almost always patient with us, beyond any reasonable expectation or merit on our part.

I am pretty sure that much of what we expect, and even more of what we imagine, about bears is beyond the limitations of human language. That is why, when we talk about bears, we say what needs saying—expressing the inexpressible, as it were—in the stories we tell. Except for those few of us gifted with artistic skills to evoke such inexpressibles in music or art, we can only resort to stories to capture the deeper essentials of what bears mean to us. This is how the grand and interminable work-in-progress of "bear-human relationships"—a phrase whose deadening flatness proves just how hard it is to get at the intangibles we share with bears—advances. And it is why I have written this book. I love and often celebrate the quantifiable realities that science brings us; such knowledge has enriched so many elements of the bear's world. But for me, at least, it comes down at last to the stories and the intangibles they celebrate.

A few years ago, introducing a collection of my previously published fishing stories entitled *The Fishing Life*, I started with this: "I'm sure there are plenty of writers whose output slips into such tidy pigeonholes that a book like this is never possible, much less necessary. Mine doesn't. For the past thirty years or so, in a perhaps naïve attempt to share the joys of the fisherman's world with everyone else, I have scattered stories about fish and fishing in books and articles that were aimed at, well, everyone else."

The same holds true for my writings about bears. Over the same years that I was writing or editing half a dozen books about bears, I was also spraying ruminations about bears into all manner of publications, including other people's anthologies, books of my own that were primarily about something else, and essays and articles in a variety of magazines and journals. But as pleased as I was to publish those pieces, I couldn't help regretting that so many of them probably slipped under the radar of readers who are especially and specifically devoted to bears and bear books.

So, inspired and emboldened in part by the kindness with which *The Fishing Life* was received, in the present book I have gathered up—from a greater quantity of material that was too dated or otherwise didn't seem to fit—my favorites among my own bear writings.

Over the forty-some years that I've been writing books, I've been fortunate to be able to revise quite a few of them for second and even third editions. The loftiest view of this revised-edition enterprise is that it allows a writer to rethink and revise his views as well as to inform readers of important changes in whatever story the book tells (a less lofty view would be that it gives the writer a rare chance to keep at it until he gets it right). The most important example in the case of my bear books is *The Bears of Yellowstone*, whose second and third editions, though coming after the first at mere six-year intervals, reported on significant developments in the fast-moving story of the science and management of those world-famous animals. I always rather intended to do a fourth edition—one more shot at getting it right—but I fear now I've waited too long. Somehow other projects always took precedence, and now even the thought of the energy and time I'd need to catch up on that vital and convoluted story, and then make sense of it in print, just brings on a pressing urge to go take a nap.

But as with the various second and third editions of my previous bear books, I appreciate the opportunity the present book affords to reconsider and rework a number of shorter bear-related works before including them here. A great joy of the memoirist's art is having the chance to compare notes with my former selves, to see if I think and feel the same way about the topics involved as I did when I first explored them in print.

And I keep exploring, which means that substantial portions of this book have not been previously published. Like most other parts of wild nature, it seems there is always another look to take, always more to say, about bears. We learn and imagine and often even decide things, then we turn back and wonder some more—perhaps somewhat fearfully, because we doubt that even today, with our magnificent scientific tool kit and our global multicultural stances, we're yet sharp enough to do justice to bears.

Thus this book's new chapters are written in the same spirit as the others, comprised of equal parts wonder over the bears that make it all possible, joy at the privilege of sharing my stories, and gratitude that you continue to read them.

This book being at heart a memoir of personal ideas, opinions, and experiences, I have tried whenever possible to use my own photographs of the places and experiences described in the text. Any other photographs, and all other illustrations, are credited individually.

The Bear
Doesn't Know

ONE

Yellowstone

Early Bears

One very early spring day, about thirty years ago, I was up on the south slopes of Mount Washburn in Yellowstone National Park with two good friends, grizzly bear researchers Marilynn and Steve French. There was still a lot of snow, which enabled us to backtrack a mating pair of grizzly bears a short distance until we found their most recently abandoned daybeds in a cozy little copse of lodgepole pines. The daybeds were just large bearish-roundish depressions in the old snow that still covered last summer's dried-out vegetation. It's amazing how exciting the least evidence of something that isn't there any more can be, and these were even more so because it hadn't been but a few hours, at most, since they'd vacated the beds. We knew they were somewhere nearby.

The story of the bears' morning was still fresh to be read in the snow. As they left the daybeds they moved uphill through a mixture of pines and snowy glades, the male following behind the female the way males do at such times. Three times in the first hundred yards, the female paused long enough to defecate. Each time, the male (who we knew from previous observations to be huge) stopped and with precision accuracy dropped a load of his own directly on top of hers.

Though we were all quite familiar with the literature of grizzly bear mating behavior, and though Marilynn and Steve had put in infinitely more observation time with mating grizzlies than I had, none of us had heard of this particular trick.

But it wasn't hard to read. It seemed pretty clear that the male was speaking in the possessive—"She's mine, don't go getting ideas"—to any other male bear that might come along and notice the droppings, whose hearty aroma would no doubt tell him an enticing story. At the time I joked that our big male's technique was quite effective. I had no desire whatsoever to offer to buy that female bear a drink.

But because the droppings, especially the male's, were so large, we began wondering about other things. For example, what if you had never seen or heard of a grizzly bear? What if you were walking through the woods and you suddenly came upon those fresh piles, or any such pile produced by the big male alone? You would instantly know what the stuff was, but what sort of creature would your imagination build around the orifice required to produce it? Your database is modest, but it gives you lots of room to wonder.

What my uninformed imagination might make of a pile of bear scat is an appealing and amusing question, but, like so many other things I notice in bear country, it leads me to harder and ultimately more enriching questions. For just one of many examples, if a grizzly bear has occasionally starred in some seriously disturbing dream of mine, what sort of god-awful thing chases a grizzly bear through *its* dreams?

This is the sort of thinking you find yourself doing when you embrace the excitement and wonder of bear country. The bear is something we see and think and dream together, our many voices and needs clashing and striving and sometimes eventually harmonizing. We encounter the bear, whether in person or in print or in any other way, and by doing so we wonder and learn and imagine and come back to wonder some more, maybe even wondering somewhat fearfully what it *ought* to mean if we were only better at taking it all in. Sensing all that demanding, exhilarating wonder-filled hope from the beginning, I have for many years now taken bears personally, living long enough—almost all my adult life—in bear country to feel both honored and obliged to struggle for something deeper than received wisdoms, headline emotions, and casual impressions.

It is in that schizophrenic and somewhat wacky spirit—"Let's all love bears! But let's keep the hell out of their way!"—that we fellow pilgrims, altogether and each on our own, wander into bear country.

I can't remember the first wild bear I ever saw, but that is not to say that I don't know where that bear was. In 1951, when I was three, we lived in Hershey, Pennsylvania. Late that summer my parents left my school-aged older brother and sister with friends and took me along on what at the time was a great car adventure: driving all the way to Miami Beach and back. This may not seem in the least notable to today's drivers, and it certainly wasn't like making a cross-country trip in your Model A Ford in the 1930s. Still, 1951 was before the modern interstate highway system was much more than a gleam in Ike's eye, and the trip provided me with my earliest dateable memories.

The most distinctive and reliable of these memories was of some place in the rural South, where my dad had to drive the family Nash across the shallow, unbridged ford of a creek. Coming from the well-paved North, this was exciting stuff, no doubt made more so by my parents making sure I was looking out the car window as the creek splashed against the rocker panels. That's the extent of the memory I have of the moment, but it was enough. Who knew cars could go in water? Who knows what I made of it right then, beyond that it was a big enough deal, a real adventure, to stick in my memory? Wild times in olden days.

What didn't stick in my memory of that trip, ironically it now seems, were the bears. On our way home we made our way to the highlands along the North Carolina–Tennessee border for a visit to Great Smoky Mountains National Park. Now a venerable cultural institution and irreplaceable world-class ecological treasure, at the time we visited the park it was only twenty-seven years old. I have no memories of this visit, so it exists in my head only as a photo of my dad and me in front of the bullet-hole-ridden park sign, and some tiny fragments of nostalgic jogs from my parents, as in, "Paul, remember when we went to the Smokies?"

1. The author and his father at Great Smoky Mountains National Park, 1951. The bullet-hole-ridden park sign perfectly symbolizes the desperate funding shortfalls and sometimes violent local animosities faced by this superb bear-country park at the time. Photo by Judith Schullery.

Nope. I don't. No doubt we saw the park's famous roadside black bears, but unlike the big Nash wallowing through that anonymous branch water, they didn't stick in my mind. Too bad, too. It would have made a nifty opening for this book if I could describe my "first" wild bear. Nor do I have any memory of the appalling tourist traps near the park, some of which routinely featured a forlorn fly-swarmed black bear chained up out front—a sadly effective tourist attractant in those days.

As it turned out, the first bear of any sort that I do remember, and still one of the most memorable, was not wild. His name was Andy, and he lived in what we would now consider a terribly small cage just a few miles from my grandparents' house in southeastern Ohio. There in Fairfield County, at a rural junction known as Weidner's Corner, there was a little gas station that over the years evolved into a locally renowned café that only finally closed down a few years ago. My family didn't move to Ohio until the early 1960s, but before that we had annual opportunities to drive by Andy's cage when we were visiting my grandparents. After we moved to Ohio in 1963, I saw him more often as I passed by either on a bicycle or in a car, and much of my early idea of what a black bear looked like, how it moved, and so on, was based on Andy. It wasn't until later that I saw how utterly different an unconstrained bear could be.

The details of Andy's story, which I've occasionally wondered about ever since, were finally chronicled to my grateful satisfaction in a splendid local newspaper article (*Lancaster Eagle Gazette*, November 13, 2016) by Joyce Harvey, to whom I owe many of the details that follow.

According to Joyce, Oscar Weidner was a longtime president of the county fish and game association. In 1948, about the time I was busy being born, Oscar was at the Ohio State Fair in nearby Columbus, where he unexpectedly accepted responsibility for a two-year-old Canadian black bear cub that had been featured in a temporary exhibit but now needed a permanent home. Andy was named for the warden who apparently was in charge of the exhibit.

Andy's cage looked so much like a jail because it was, having been built from the leftovers of a former jail in another nearby town. It was just a heavy rectangular cage that featured a bunkerlike concrete shelter for Andy to curl up in. I suppose but don't know that he may have slept through some colder parts of winters and spent the rest of his days sitting, standing, or pacing in his small cage. When I was five, or ten, or even fifteen, it is unlikely that I gave much thought to what a tragically limited existence this was for a profoundly opportunistic omnivore whose every urge was to wander daily through nature's smorgasbord. But then this was back in the era of unregulated roadside zoos all over America, many of which were simply awful. By those low standards, Andy had it better than most.

Given that disheartening limitation, I can still enjoy Joyce's story of Andy's diet, which though hardly "healthy" in the modern sense, at least suggests the extent to which he was part of the neighborhood and had even been taken into the hearts of his neighbors: "They fed Andy dog food and vegetables, but [Oscar's son]

Tom remembers Hostess cupcakes were his favorite food. Hostess delivery people saved outdated cupcakes and other goodies to bring to Andy."

At this point in the story my own memories intrude. My uncles and my older brother Steve were all serious fishermen, and among their quarry there in warm-water Ohio were the big carp of nearby Buckeye Lake. While most of the people we knew, including all the members of my immediate family, considered carp inedible, we did know a few people with a taste for them, so the carp that the family's anglers brought home from the lake did have some meaningful destinations and weren't just tossed in the garbage. As I've been writing this I checked in with Steve to compare our memories, and he tells me that carp were also regarded as fine fertilizer and were sometimes buried under one of Grandma's apple trees.

But Andy was also an outlet for such carp largesse. One day I rode along with my brother and an uncle or two to take a several-pound carp to Andy. Someone, not me, tossed it onto the top of Andy's cage, where he could reach it and pull it through the bars. I checked with Steve about this occasion and, I suppose unsurprisingly, we have somewhat different memories of it.

I remember that once Andy had the carp in paw, he put it on the cement floor of his cage, planted a foot firmly on one end (seems to me it was the head), and used his other paw to peel back the skin and flank the whole length of the fish. Steve, who was five years older and therefore probably the more trustworthy witness, especially remembers "the loud crunch as he took the first bite into it." Perhaps both memories are just different parts of the same event. The mention of the crunch resonates clearly for me, because many years later I would hear its match as I watched Alaskan brown bears consume salmon.

As for Andy's diet, I am retroactively embarrassed to read, in Joyce Harvey's account of his career as a roadside attraction, that "Though fishermen brought him fish from Buckeye Lake, too many fish made him ill." Oops.

Overall, his diet apparently agreed with him. Joyce says he eventually reached five hundred pounds in weight, though I can't say I remember ever seeing him that big. I wish I had, though it's even sadder to think of a bear that huge spending all his time in such a tiny space.

Fast-forward to December of 1978, when I was more or less a grownup living in Vermont, and my mother sent me a local clipping with Andy's obituary, which, in yet another indication of how fond we all were of him, made the front page of the county's leading newspaper: "Weidner's Corner gas station near Baltimore is without a familiar face today. Andy the Bear, an attraction at the crossroads of Ohio 37 and 256 for 30 years, died Sunday."

He was buried next to his cage, which was eventually torn down, but the last time I passed through the junction his blockish little concrete shelter was still there by its tree, looking odd and out of place in the vacant yard but also looking stubbornly resistant to all but the most determined and explosive of demolition strategies.

I must have seen other bears during my childhood, if only in the zoos my family might have visited, but until I was in my early twenties if anyone had mentioned "bear" to me, Andy most likely would have come to mind first.

The good news for me was that Andy and any others among those first ones were followed by others, here and there, big and small, tame and wild, real and cartoon, seen and dreamt, gradually resolving into clearer and clearer memories. My personal best news of all is that, as of 1972, when I first became a ranger-naturalist in Yellowstone National Park, the whole bear inquiry was abruptly elevated from a casual and largely accidental matter of interest to very near the center of my universe. From then on, the bears have been an important and often urgent matter, my own growing number of observations complemented and enriched by the teachings of many much-more-learned friends and by a vast, compelling, and still eager reading of the immense popular and scientific literature of bears. I'm delighted to say, now that my seventieth birthday is receding into dimming memory, that the bears keep showing up, and I continue to be enchanted by their presence in my world.

The Bear Doesn't Know

There is no trail to the pond. It lies, unnamed as far as I know, in a flat alpine saddle in northwestern Yellowstone National Park, between Gray and Little Quadrant Peaks—a perfect mountain meadow almost never visited by people. There are a few whitebark pine trees, and the whole little plain, just a few acres, is quite level. The pond is toward the north end; it may be spring fed, or it may just get its water from rain and snow melt from the surrounding mountain walls. The elevation is near nine thousand feet. I doubt that the place is as warmly hospitable most of the year as we found it that day in early September.

We'd been told that we could leave the Fawn Pass Trail, to the south, and ride over the saddle by following animal trails and meadows. It's not possible to get lost, with the surrounding mountains serving as such unmistakable landmarks, but I was still a little edgy about such an extended bushwhack. Horses need a lot more space than hikers, and except for the meadow, this was steep country.

The pond has a tiny overflow on its east end. The trickle goes a few yards and turns northward, dropping into a forested ravine. The ravine was our recommended avenue north, but it was mostly untrailed. We soon had the horses hopping and sloshing back and forth over the stream, seeking the least troublesome course. Too often to suit us, we could only travel in the little streambed itself; steep banks and deadfall kept us pinned there, and the horses slipped and lurched along the wet, rocky streambed.

We didn't notice tributaries, but they were there. Within a mile of the pond the rivulet was a genuine creek, tumbling and twisting over logs and rocks and making passage even more difficult for the horses. At one point a ragged, pointed length of lodgepole pine deadfall branch extended out over a narrow spot in the creek, and I watched helplessly as it scraped along the flank of my companion's horse as they splashed by. Luckily it wasn't firmly anchored in the streamside soil and it flexed and twisted away rather than digging into the horse.

Then, seeking safer trails for the horses, we climbed the east slope of the ravine for some distance above the stream, so far that its noise was inaudible. While moving through fairly open timber on a gentler slope, we heard a large animal crashing through the brush and deadfall ahead of us. My companion, riding ahead of me, got a glimpse of the animal. "I think we scared up a bear."

I was skeptical. We'd been jumping elk for two days, and one large animal can sound pretty much like another when it's running frightened in heavy timber.

Traditional wisdom has it that a surprised bear, like many animals, will often flee until it locates a good spot from which to check out what frightened it. About 150 yards farther along, my companion pointed up the slope to our right. "There's the bear."

She stopped her horse, and as I caught up I saw an adequately large grizzly about fifty yards off, standing on his hind legs. He was watching us from the edge of a tight stand of lodgepole pines.

My companion asked, "Should we take his picture?" just as the bear seemed to decide something; he came down on all fours and took a step down the hill toward us.

"No, the horses haven't seen him yet, and I think we'd better just keep going."

We rode quickly out of his sight, but within a few minutes we were rimrocked by a sharp side ravine off the main creek, and we had to retrace our steps back past where we'd seen the bear. He was gone, and we moved on down to the stream and continued north.

The horses amazed us that way. On this trip they plodded past any number of elk and coyotes, and one moose we encountered, at about thirty feet away, without any sign of noticing. We heard but did not see bighorn sheep; their tenor baaing at least got Midget to perk up his ears. On several occasions bull elk, getting in voice for later recreations, bugled hoarsely from the slopes above us. The horses plodded on.

But of all that trip—the echoes of elk bugles ringing across the stone walls, the stark, lawn-like alpine meadows, the midnight mountains half lost in star shadow, a golden eagle soaring off the point of Gray Peak, and all the rest—that moment near the bear lingers most persistently in my memory. I've relived that encounter hundreds of times, chasing it around in my mind, picking at it for detail or depth and often finding them; running those frames through the projector, editing, enhancing, and embellishing them without consciously wanting or needing to. The bear came down on all fours. He—we both made him male in our minds—watched us until he knew we saw him. He decided something. He came down on all fours and took a step forward. He decided something, he came down on all fours and took a step forward down the hill and into my soul.

That, I had often been told, is the way to see your grizzly—a chance meeting on his doorstep. Whether in a moment's glance or through a morning of distant observations, you must see him at home. The time it takes to see a grizzly, the waiting involved, makes it an event long before it happens. Anticipation and romance crowd into your consciousness so that you may worry, while you're "getting ready," that the bear will somehow disappoint (which isn't possible), or that you will somehow be inadequate and will fail to enjoy, or comprehend, or be adequately enriched by the encounter. That is probably not possible either, if only because once you have realized just how special the event is your subconscious will take care of making the experience memorable. Like your first kiss or shaking hands with the president, it is memorable even if it went wrong.

And, appropriately, the bear doesn't know; it all means so much to you, but the bear disregards it almost right away; not forgetting where the encounter occurred, but hardly as thrilled or impressed with it as you were.

Since the 1890s, until recently, you could see your Yellowstone grizzly bear a lot more easily, and a lot less appropriately, at a garbage dump. In the 1960s those few people who knew somebody who could get them into the Trout Creek dump (not near public roads and off-limits except to researchers and park officials) were likely to see anywhere from twenty to a few dozen grizzly bears at once, a visual overload I have trouble imagining and am just as glad I can't share, because these dozens of bears were all up to their appetites in garbage.

Feeding Yellowstone's grizzlies at dumps both inside and near the park was just as much an institution as feeding the black bears along the roads, and feeding the black bears was the most desired of all visitor experiences for millions of people. In 1962 my parents brought us to Yellowstone, and a small black bear tried to eat my sister's camera (or my sister; we never were sure). What I've seen in Yellowstone has convinced me that feeding wild bears, in dumps or along roads, is a stupid, ugly, typically human thing to do. What bothers me most is not so much the people who get hurt but what it does to the bears. Hundreds of people were clawed or scratched in those days (the black bears did some mean work on a few, but most were just scratched and scared), but look what those people were doing: ignoring all sorts of warnings; insisting on getting between mothers and cubs; feeding bears film wrappers, cigarette butts, ice cubes, cherry bombs, and even food; running over an occasional cub . . . in short, doing everything to test the forbearance of an incredibly patient providence. Providence frequently took the form of a mama black bear who finally had too much and took a swat at the hundredth citizen of Poughkeepsie to make a grab at her cubs that day. Then the rangers would be called to destroy the "dangerous bear." The rangers, who were in on the problem and yet preferred the company of bears much of the time, ended up destroying dozens of bears. Life is not simple, even for idyllic types like rangers and bears.

The rangers knew the bears shouldn't be fed. It had been illegal since 1902. The tourists did, too; a survey conducted in 1953, when the great Yellowstone "bear jams" were beginning to reach their mile-long, radiator-boiling peak, revealed that 95 percent of the people knew they were breaking the law when they fed bears. Only the bears didn't know. Being bears, extraordinarily adaptive omnivores, they were simply cashing in on an obvious good thing. The Rocky Mountain Free Lunch. Dill pickles, Twinkies, ham on rye . . . the wilderness was never like this.

The only difference at the dumps was that servers and served were more select groups. Park employees, researchers, and a chosen few dignitary-gawkers were privy audience to lunchtime for one of North America's most spectacular evolutionary achievements, the grizzly bear. But, I am happy to say, this culinary Camelot was also doomed.

Even after so much modern scientific study, and especially now that they're not eating garbage, bear's food habits still surprise us. In the 1970s a Yellowstone grizzly was seen passing up easily available dead meat to hunt and kill elk of its own. Even the carcass feeders are still teaching us. For a very long time, outdoorsy common knowledge had it that bears of both species were "foul feeders," that "them bears don't get really worked up about a carcass until it's good and ripe." Actually, no one has proved that bears have a taste preference for rotten meat over fresh meat, but practically speaking, a rotting carcass has to be a lot easier for a bear to sniff out than a new one. For that reason they may feed more on the rank ones. They may also prefer a rank carcass because it will contain more maggots, a bear delicacy. What bears need and what people find disgusting tell us more about people than it does about bears. As the beggar and dump bears most dishearteningly demonstrated, willingness to try new foods is the bear's special blessing; even were the animal able to do so, it could not afford to worry that its diet causes people to suspect a character deficiency. Maggots, escargot; rancid elk meat, buttermilk; who's really deficient here?

And that's the whole thing with bears, isn't it? Our millennia-long cultural, religious, scientific, and personal struggles to come to terms with the differences and similarities between humans and all the other animals constitute one of the great sagas of science and philosophy. Though it was for many centuries fashionable—more often than not for the most self-serving of reasons—to imagine all our fellow creatures as emotionally and mentally enfeebled life forms, most of us don't go for that simple a view any more. Especially in a national park setting, where it is fairly easy to practice a more neutral stance, we're apt to agree with naturalist Andrew Skutch, who pointed out that, "We feel more comfortable in a world enlivened by beings akin to us in mind, as in anatomy and physiology, than in one in which we are lonely exceptions." Skutch was writing specifically about birds at the time, but if we have gotten "comfortable" relating in deep ways to the mind of a chickadee, how much easier must it be for us similarly to connect with a bear?

It was during my early years in Yellowstone, and ironically while watching a bear die, that I received what may still be the most telling lesson I've ever had in why we are so unable to keep our minds straight when it comes to bears.

The 1970s were sensationally touchy times in the Yellowstone bear saga, as the grizzly bear population was controversially small. Though the various parties who were just then arguing over exactly how low the numbers were—a little, a lot, or circling-the drain hopeless—no position holders were casual about even a single bear death.

But the hard truth was that once a bear was recognized as "incorrigible," it had to go. Incorrigibility was defined by certain specific standards having mostly to do with how many chances a bear had been given to stop getting into trouble or posing a danger to people. And though even the definition of incorrigibility itself was also a debatable moving target, eventually the day came when a bear simply ran out of chances and managers simply ran out of choices (giving such bears to zoos was not always an option).

When a bear got into trouble, typically in a campground or other developed area, rangers would trap it and, depending upon several factors (black bears, for example, were rarely hauled very far), haul it off to some other part of the park or surrounding wildlands and let it go. It was both a great evolutionary advantage and a tragic practical disadvantage to the bears that they were often astonishingly good and dismayingly quick at finding their way back over dozens of miles of rough, unfamiliar country to wherever they'd been trapped—which goes a long way toward explaining why sometimes they ran out of chances. There were grizzly bears for whom the entire Greater Yellowstone Ecosystem, some eighteen million acres—give or take—of national parks, forests, and other public lands, was not large enough to prevent their promptly finding their way back from wherever they were taken.

Such a bear, a male, inadvertently provided me with a startling and unforgettable lesson in the complications of thinking clearly, carefully, and compassionately about these bewildering, wondrous animals. His death occurred along a gravel lane on a suitably secluded hillside near park headquarters. The bear was being held in one of the ubiquitous culvert traps—a hefty metal tube about twelve feet long and four feet across, made from a section of corrugated culvert mounted on a frame with a pair of wheels and a tow bar. These traps were the essence of serviceable function. Bears were baited into them with a variety of rank treats in a bucket suspended from the interior roof well inside the culvert; when the bear climbed in and started messing with the bucket, it triggered the drop of the trap's heavy door and was caught. These big traps were and are routinely used to haul a bear to any roaded location in the park, or loaded onto a boat or suspended under a helicopter for more remote translocations. (Among its many other attractions, the late Jerry Mernin's classic memoir *Yellowstone Ranger* contains many stirring and instructive accounts of the use of these traps).

By the late 1970s, sensitized by years of wild accusations of bear slaughters in the earlier days of the bear-management controversy, Yellowstone's managers, rangers, and biologists jumped through a reasonable set of formal, procedural hoops when killing and documenting the death of each bear. But it was not normally done with much of an audience, so I couldn't say how or why it turned out that I was there for this sad moment; I can't imagine I had any official role to play. By that point in my work in the park it sometimes just happened that I ended up being one of the okay people to have around. In any event, and though it sounds odd when I say it about such an occasion, looking back now I can see that whatever got me there, it was to my great advantage, both professionally and personally, that I showed up.

The process was utterly unceremonious, but it still felt at every stage that something momentous was happening. Looked at in cold mathematical terms, I was witnessing the regrettable reduction of an already stressed and reduced grizzly bear population. On the grander scale and longer haul of what brought this species onto the world stage—Canadian ecologist Steve Herrero eloquently characterized the grizzly bear as "a massive and powerful statement of the evolutionary history of circumpolar northern environments"—I was witnessing the destruction of a magnificent force of nature. If you can separate out such complicated responses to such an event, good for you. I can't.

Unobserved by the bear, a member of the Interagency Grizzly Bear Study Team quietly—and it all happened quietly—reached a large hypodermic needle into a small opening on the side of the culvert trap and administered a lethal injection into the bear's broad flank. It succumbed in moments, lapsing into unconsciousness and then death with only a few quiet shivers and jerks. Once dead, it was pulled from the trap, spread-eagled on its back upon a tarp, and skinned.

And here was the sudden surprise, and the lasting illumination of the day for me. As the skinner separated the last of the hide from the carcass, I experienced a shock of recognition I was later to hear about again and again in the bear lore, especially in the old-time accounts of bear hunters. When a bear's hide is removed, and what's left lies stretched out there, it looks very much like a dead man, a grotesque, heavy-framed, humanlike thing. If at that point in the affair we are paying attention at all, we are uncomfortably reminded of ourselves, just as when we watch living bears we are struck by the mysteries and consequences of the gulf that separates us from all the species who are at our mercy.

But I have to tell you that a dead bear's skinned carcass brings an immediacy to the enterprise of understanding bears that I have never otherwise felt during all the time I've spent watching the living ones, much less during the years I've spent reading, talking, and thinking about them when they weren't in view. The differences between that bear carcass and a human body seemed trivial, and yet stupendous. I can only hope I never get over it.

In the late 1960s and early 1970s, during the early stirrings of the modern environmental movement and as national parks were undergoing a heated and institutionally straining self-appraisal over their most meaningful mission, Yellowstone officials cut off the gravy train. They stopped roadside feeding of bears and they closed the open-pit garbage dumps. The dumps had been frequented by grizzly bears for more than eighty years, and their closing caused a monstrous national controversy, with political influence, scientific careers, both well-contained and outrageous egos, and the bears' welfare all at stake. By 1977 bears were still getting garbage here and there near the park, but only one dump remained open in the park, a small scar near the north entrance, used by the town of Gardiner, Montana. Through a long-standing agreement between the Park Service and the town, this dump was a part of the community's way of life. For all the usual political and practical reasons, it was more difficult to close this dump, which serviced a private community, than it was to close the others, which serviced only park facilities. In every case, something else had to be done with the garbage, and it was harder to convince a small border town to spend the extra money than it was to organize better garbage disposal in the park.

Everyone knew the dump would have to be closed eventually. Not only was it unnaturally influencing the movements of the neighborhood bears, not only was it a flagrant violation of EPA standards; it was a fabulously disgusting sight, even as dumps go.

For good reasons, someone in the park hierarchy realized that it would be useful, both scientifically and politically, to know more about the bears who used this dump. It was common knowledge that on most nights there were a few grizzlies at the dump, only a mile or so from town. Kids shot at them with .22s. Grown-ups (ha!) drove around the locked gate at the main road and went down the old service road to the dump so they could sit in their cars and watch the bears. But nobody could say how many different bears there were, or how many of them were grizzlies, or if any sported radio collars or ear tags from the Interagency Grizzly Bear Study Team. Bears can roam great distances, so knowing how many use what areas is essential information when determining the size, health, and fate of the population.

A few biologists and rangers began taking turns monitoring the dump. Sometime after 10:00 p.m., we'd unlock the gate, drive in, lock it behind us and drive the dirt road to where it passed behind a rise and ended at the dump. We'd sit there an hour or so, trying to identify individuals by their tags, size, colors, and other markings. Sows with young were regarded as especially important components of the population. Bears are nearly as individual as people in appearance, but very few of us get to see them often enough to get to know what to look for. I never got any good at it on my all-too-few visits to the dump, though years later, while watching various wild bears, I did a little better.

The first visit was my worst. I'd only been to the dump once before, in daylight, so I didn't have a very good fix on the setting. The forested slopes of the Gallatin Mountains, specifically Sepulcher Mountain and Electric Peak, rise steeply into the Yellowstone River Valley on the park boundary. Between the river and the mountains is a narrow shelf, actually a rolling flat, mostly bare of trees, about half a mile wide. In a hollow, between a low ridge and the base of the mountains, sat the dump. Well, it didn't really sit; it sort of festered. It was perfectly accessible to the bears who roamed the extremely rough country in the Gallatins. It occurs to me today, more than forty years later, that the grizzly bear we saw that day, deep in the wilderness near Fawn Pass, could easily have also been an occasional patron of the Gardiner dump. I wouldn't doubt he knew about it.

That first evening, as we rounded the rise and bounced along into the dump, Les played the spotlight across the footslopes of the mountain to our left, locking onto four or five brown bear bottoms as they galloped over the ridge into a gulch.

"The engine scares them away. They come back in twenty minutes or so."

We parked at the very end of the road, engine and lights off, with garbage dump on three sides and a small bare hill immediately to our right. The car sat on a little earth ramp that extended out into the portion of the dump then in use, but off to our left and behind us stretched several acres of American Fantasia: washing machines and couches, cellophane and freezer wrapper, detergent boxes and tin cans—the broken, the rusty, and the disposable.

"They usually come in through that draw." Les pointed straight ahead to the far side of the clutter, where the hillside split into two humps with a gap between them. "Sometimes they come right over that hill," he continued, pointing to my right, "and right past your side of the car." I voted for the draw.

Fifteen minutes later, our eyes now fully accustomed to the weak moonlight and our ears searching the night for sounds (a rat scrambling over a pile of tin cans makes a noise a lot like a grizzly bear would make when you're expecting a grizzly bear), Les pointed at the draw. "There's one."

Later, I had time to realize that my brief daytime visit to the dump had left me with a poor notion of its size. In the flat moonlight my eyes had misplaced the draw about twice as far away as it really was. So, laboring under this significant misimpression, I saw a bear twice as large as a bear should be. "God, lookit how big!" Eloquence under pressure is natural to the experienced woodsman.

Les didn't answer. I assumed he was as agog as I was, but when I looked over he wasn't even watching. He was calmly taking notes—his clipboard resting on the steering wheel—about the bear's arrival. I squirmed and gaped. The bear lumbered silently down the draw toward the dump (and us), casting a moon shadow like the Astrodome. This bear wasn't large; this bear was vast.

Before long, he placed himself in a helpful context. He wandered past an old ice box and didn't dwarf it nearly as much as I would have expected. I then realized that I'd been seeing wrong, and that he was a reasonable grizzly bear after all, maybe three hundred or three hundred and fifty pounds. Les recognized him as a boar who had been seen there before—a little lean, a little ratty, he looked like he'd slept in his clothes.

Most of the others we saw, on that and subsequent nights, were sleek and fat. It isn't always true that a partial diet of garbage makes bears sick, but among other problems it may increase the risk of natural sickness as essentially solitary animals get together in big groups where diseases that might normally be restricted to one can be transmitted to many.

Before long the boar was joined by a family group of sow with two young of the year. A coyote skirted the place nervously, almost seeming to need the company more than the food.

I suppose that the scientists on the famous Craighead team, who spent years studying the dump bears in the 1960s, got to the point where every moment of watching wasn't a thrill, but I hadn't spent years at it, and the excitement didn't wear off. Even after an hour or so of watching them, there was always a gut-tightening surge of adrenaline when a new one wandered close, or when a giant head suddenly loomed up directly in front of the car (one ranger who made his first trip with me later couldn't get over the size of the heads; whenever I'd pick up the clipboard he'd tell me to "make sure you say that they have really large heads").

And watching them, just sitting there watching them feed, was enchanting. Sorting through the junk (one imagines the bear casually pitching a refrigerator over his shoulder, but most of the sorting was of a more delicate type), poking a claw through some wet paper (Did I miss any lettuce here last night?), or strolling along swaying that big head back and forth, the bear is just like any other open-minded shopper. Is this detergent good in cold water? Are the tomatoes fresh? Do the coupons apply to the day-old bread? No, you can't have that, I saw it first. There is so much curiosity, so much of the small boy picking up pretty rocks, that you quickly begin to see personhood in the bear. Or you begin to see bearhood in yourself.

They can get used to the same things, too: cans with sharp edges, rubbery vegetables, a table too close to the kitchen, fire.

Fire? Yes, fire, the great Bad Guy of countless children's animal stories of earlier days (along with Nasty Hunters and Wolves). It seemed that some of the stuff the dump received every day was burnable, and desultory efforts to light it usually left a couple of hot spots at night. The bears pawed all around the flames, their noses so close they'd reflect orange. I understand that this happens at other bear dumps, and occasionally a careless bear gets too close and gets burned or singed. Adaptive omnivores indeed.

On the theory that in a place like Yellowstone it's always better to have a camera than to not have a camera, I'd brought along my good one. It was obviously not good enough to take a discernible picture in the absence of light, so Les and I made a few tries at spotlight photos of individual bears. Certainly such pictures could have been helpful officially for identifying individuals, but in my heart I knew that I was just succumbing to the fundamental touristic impulse of pointing a camera at anything really cool. Les rolled down his window so he could swing the car's spotlight around to aim it at a bear, and I'd bang away with the little Pentax. The bears seemed unconcerned about being in the spotlight, but the pictures of the more distant bears were so dull and grainy as to be useless except as yes-I-was-actually-there memory joggers. We did get one bear as it passed right in front of the car, just a sidelong profile with a big shoulder and long snout, but still a vivid reminder of how close we were.

Another time a supervisor asked us to satisfy his curiosity about a popular product then being touted in magazines as a good defense against wild animals. It was an air horn, one of those little cannisters that otherwise sensible people used to blast into your ear at football games. People were apparently being suckered into buying them as protection against grizzly bears. If a bear charges you, just toot this thing at him and he'll run away. Sounds great, I'll take two.

People who believe that a good loud noise is sure to scare a grizzly bear away can't be people who have ever listened to grizzly bears making loud noises at one another. A loud noise, especially if the bear hasn't been having such a good day or is just in the mood to swap loud noises with someone, doesn't seem like a good way to protect yourself. Who knows what the bear will think about it?

2. By no means great photographic art—a technically poor photo, in fact—but its having been taken by the author in the middle of the night over the hood of a ranger patrol car makes this a good picture, and a great memory. Photo by author.

There's a lot to be said for loud noises when you're hiking. If you make them as you walk along you're much less likely to surprise some animal that's sleeping in the middle of the trail; most animals move off a ways if they hear you coming. But once you've surprised one, and it's checking you out on its hind legs or ambling toward you for a closer look (or worse), you might as well count on divine intervention as make a loud noise at it. Either might work, but I bet that if God does intervene He won't use an air horn.

Anyway, Les and I waited until there was a sow, about two hundred and fifty pounds or so, with a big yearling about half her size, right in front of the car. They were just getting involved in a huge pile of radishes (I can't imagine how anyone could come to have so many radishes as this to throw away at once), no more than thirty feet from the steering wheel. It was dark, and I wondered aloud at how *I* would react if someone cut loose behind my back with one of those horns at a time and place like this. The bears were chowing down with some enthusiasm when Les, in the driver's seat, stuck the can out the window and gave it a short, piercing toot. Both bears gave a start, then resumed eating.

"Hmm. Not much response." We were whispering.

"No. Maybe you should try a longer blast." Les nodded, held the can out the window, and pressed the button for several seconds. At this point the patrol car windshield seemed to be about as much protection as my Audubon Society membership. Les, a calm, sensible man, had his service revolver in his other hand, just in case the air horn said something horribly insulting in bear talk, but the revolver didn't look up to stopping a grizzly bear if one decided to come through the windshield.

Luckily, bears are patient, and though they don't know that rangers are their friends, they don't seem to give a lot of conscious thought to how much damage they can do, either. The second blast definitely disturbed them, because they stopped eating. They both looked around at the dark car. I was never sure what the bears thought of the car, or if they could see us well through the windshield, or if they knew that cars usually have people in them (I don't know as much as bears don't know). These two, after a minute of checking us out, wandered away. Either they were restless, or annoyed, or tired of the radishes, or something else. I couldn't say for sure, but the air horn wasn't very convincing.

At the time of my dump duty, outdoor writers were getting a lot of mileage out of talking about bear repellents that were "proven effective" in some hunting camp or other. Paradichlorobenzene (moth balls) was mentioned frequently as a good bear repellent. Yellowstone rangers had checked this out by putting some out in one of the park dumps—and thus got to watch grizzly bears *eating* paradichlorobenzene.

That said, even in the 1970s a number of scientists were working very hard to come up with effective "aversive agents" that might lessen the risk of harm when humans and bears encounter one another. At that time I—perhaps naïvely, maybe even self-righteously—viewed the development of aversive agents as a necessary evil. I did understand that with so many people insisting on crowding into bear country there had to be a way to keep the injury rate as low as possible, if only so the bears wouldn't get a lot of bad publicity and end up being killed off. Okay, I conceded, we need some device or other for this purpose. But I was still a bit reluctant to compromise my lofty wilderness ideals no matter how unkind their real-world implications. In the first edition of *The Bears of Yellowstone* (1980), I confidently asserted that, "perhaps someday there will be something you wear, spray, eat, or sing that will guarantee your safety. In a way it would be a shame, since an important and humbling part of the grizzly country experience is that sharpening of the senses—the tuning-in on one's surroundings—that it brings out."

It's easy to think things like that when you're young and immortal. I still believe with my whole heart that it's important to protect and respect bear-country humility, but otherwise I've completely changed my mind on aversives. In the decades since my early experiences in the park—and thanks to the heroic work of a few biologists and entrepreneurs—aerosol capsaicin-based sprays have piled up an extraordinary track record for saving human lives by dissuading attacking bears. During the many years when I again worked in Yellowstone, starting in the late 1980s and onward, I and pretty much all my colleagues in the National Park Service never hiked without a cannister in a holster on our belt or pack strap. It's absolutely the right thing to do.

If you're unaware of modern bear spray—which is pretty hard to be these days, so universally appreciated is it—I urge you to study up. Read the latest brochures on bear safety issued by the management agencies who oversee bears and hikers. Track down the statistical analyses that continue to reinforce the wisdom of carrying bear spray. Read the relevant pages in the new (2018) edition of Steve Herrero's classic *Bear Attacks: Their Causes and Avoidance* (celebrated in chapter 10); you should read this book anyway. If you're going to hike in Yellowstone, the best thing to do is to go to Yellowstone National Park's official website, where you will find the latest word on the whole bear safety–human safety matter.

To all this excellent professional advice now available about bear spray, I will only offer a few reinforcing thoughts of my own. Bear

3. Then-Yellowstone chief of public affairs Marsha Karle demonstrating the effective range of a canister of bear spray. Photo by author.

spray has very often helped people—saving them from horrible or fatal injury—when they were being attacked. That's great and wonderful, but it's still better to hike so carefully and mindfully that you don't get attacked. An often-expressed concern among bear experts is that carrying bear spray might make you feel so secure that you stop paying attention to what's going on around you. As the experts say, this stuff isn't "brains in a can." Just as you can still get struck by lightning, crushed under a falling tree, or smothered in an avalanche you can, indeed, still get killed by a bear.

In the early 1990s, when I conducted a Yellowstone Institute class on bears, I invited Kerry Gunther, the park's lead bear-management biologist, to demonstrate the spray. Kerry is, by the way, another person whose many publications on bears you should read every chance you get, starting with the incomparable book edited by P. J. White, Kerry Gunther, and Frank T. van Manen, *Yellowstone Grizzly Bears: Ecology and Conservation of an Icon of Wildness* (Yellowstone National Park: Yellowstone Forever and the U.S. Geological Survey, 2017).

Anyway, Kerry's demonstration was a revelation to my institute students. As powerful as the cannisters are, my students (adults of all ages) were surprised at how short a distance the spray went (typical comment: "Well, that's thirty bucks I won't spend"). Thirty feet, or whatever distance the cannister's label may say is its effective range, really doesn't look like much out in the open, especially if you imagine a large disturbed grizzly bear glaring at you across the sagebrush at that distance. But that's a vitally important thing to keep in mind as a bear approaches with apparent aggression in mind. Unlike a firearm, this is not a long-distance weapon.

For years there, if you wanted to get to know how bear spray worked, you just bought an extra cannister and tried it out. Now that you can acquire "inert" bear spray, you can practice without any risk to yourself, but I still want to make sure you understand how dangerous a blast of the real capsaicin spray can be—to you as well as to the bear. If you spray it incautiously, you can easily find yourself painfully amazed at how the slightest wayward breeze can blow a tiny bit of spray back toward you, or toward others standing a lot more than thirty feet away. I speak from stupid personal experience when I say that you don't want to have this little lesson in how shockingly awful it is for the bear into whose eyes you might eventually spray it. *Be careful!*

And even after spraying it, you have at least one more perilous opportunity to regret doing so. As soon as possible once you're finished with the cannister, *Go wash your hands!* If you don't, the next time you happen to touch your face or rub your eyes you will again get a deeply disappointing hint of what this stuff does to a bear. You don't want to know.

Even though the availability of inert spray makes it unnecessary to practice with real capsaicin spray, I mention these cautions because they will be even more urgently important if you've just successfully sprayed a bear out on the trail. Under such high-stress, adrenaline-saturated circumstances, it will be hard to remember to be careful with that cannister in your hands, but try really hard to do so. It would be a miserable shame, and potentially a disaster, to disable yourself after the spray has done its real job.

So get an inert cannister and try it out. Practice getting it out of its holster and removing its safety clip so that you can do it smoothly and promptly. Spray it into, against, and crosswise of the wind. Have someone else spray it while you stand well off to the side—or just make a video of it—so you can see how far it goes under different circumstances.

An essential part of the expert advice that wasn't so well understood by hikers in bear spray's early days is that you should keep spraying. This isn't like firing individual shots from a weapon and then stopping to see what effect they've had; you're hoping to create a good cloud of spray between you and the bear. If the bear comes through that undeterred, keep spraying at its face until it turns away.

Last, judging from how many people are known to have completely misunderstood bear spray, I'd better say this. Bear spray is not like bug spray; spray it at the bear, *but not on anything else.* Bear-spray folklore tells us that quite a few people have bought it thinking that it works like mosquito repellent and have thus sprayed it either on themselves, their tents, their children, or something else that it didn't help and might have harmed. *Don't do that!*

Though I learned a lot from the bears at the dump, watching those grizzlies feed, search, nap, and occasionally square off for a few therapeutic loud noises, my basic convictions about the bear were only strengthened. Most basic of all is my belief that even though grizzly bears are capable of explosive devastation, they can be lived with in places like Yellowstone. They are very easy on us. Here is an animal that can bite through your skillet, or dismantle your recreational vehicle (removing the side nearest the refrigerator), or kill an elk with a good swat (ask yourself how many times you'd have to hit an elk with your hand to kill it), or reduce a dead tree to sawdust to get some ants, and it hardly ever *kills* anybody. Grizzlies can kill people, and we give them plenty of chances the way we crowd into their country. But they continue to show a restraint that amazes me—and that on my darkest days I doubt that we deserve.

I don't underestimate them, and I've had my share of memorable dreams involving me, a grizzly bear or two, and small crowded

4. The magic of wildlife watching in Yellowstone is in seeing these animals in their greater context rather than right outside the car window along the road. Photo by author.

places. Being mauled by a grizzly bear has always struck me as one of those wilderness experiences where the novelty wears off almost right away. But look at what the bears put up with: all the thousands of sweet- or sour-smelling, careless, bacon-frying hikers who intrude on them for every one "incident" (an unfortunate euphemism that probably can't be avoided) that results in human tragedy. Like a nuclear reactor, or a heart, we take the grizzly bear for granted until it does something we weren't expecting. I think, in the bear's case at least, that the problem is in our expectations, not in the bear's behavior.

We certainly make too much of the presumed "viciousness" of grizzly bears. Any species that survives in part by eating its neighbors is bound to make the community jumpy, but keep in mind that much of the time bears do no more than eat their neighbor's lawn, or dig up his flower bed.

Partly because in modern America being killed and eaten by a wild animal is incredibly rare, and partly because such an event is great press, we have a distorted view of the ferocity of grizzly bears. Every precaution must be taken—I always carry some honest fear into grizzly country—but let's be realistic about what the grizzly bear is and isn't.

The grizzly *isn't* a man-eater in the traditional sense. Unlike the famous lions and leopards of Africa or the tigers of India, the grizzly doesn't make its living eating people (a population of brown bears once got reasonably good at it in an isolated part of Russia, but even then, relatively few people were killed). Some of those historic big cats killed more than a hundred people *each*. A century ago, when Jim Corbett was hunting down man-eaters in the Kumaon Hills of India, he wasn't just some rich white hunter off on a sporting jaunt. He was a national hero. Those defenseless people were being dragged from large, settled villages, nightly, by tigers that lived in good part on human flesh.

Rare is the grizzly bear that has killed more than one person. Before 1900, some bears became famous as stock killers, but even then, some profitable exaggeration occurred to the advantage of aggrieved stockmen. Yes, both grizzly bears and black bears can and do kill people, and once in a while eat them, and even less once in a while kill them to eat them, but not as a matter of habit. Be it ever thus, please.

A friend of mine once outbluffed a young grizzly. She was hiking alone when the bear rushed toward her, apparently interested in dinner. She waved her arms, growled all manner of foul insults, and informed the bear in her biggest voice that he must understand that she was larger and meaner than he and was in no way to be considered dinner. Each of his charges was met and stopped by a louder and more blustery one by her. Each time the bear backed off, just unsure enough of himself to chicken out. She doesn't remember how many charges there were, but knowing her normal calm, I wish I could have been there. She's gifted with language, and I would have loved to hear her when *really* inspired. The bear finally went away.

Friends of mine have seen bison, or elk, or their own horses, grazing in the same meadow with a bear, just reinforcing something I'd read in Andy Russell's classic *Grizzly Country* (1967):

> Several times in Alaska we have seen caribou, dall sheep, and grizzly bears all grazing on the same slope like so many cattle. Even our pack horses pay little attention to them in the Rockies of western Canada. On two occasions I have seen a grizzly feeding with my horses. While a certain discretion is practiced by the ruminants and the horses, there is a mutual minding of one's own business that gives no indication of the stresses usually associated between a predator and prey.

Apparently there are also times when the predator only preys when the prey "acts like dinner," that is, runs or panics. A ranger I know once saw a grizzly charge an unsuspecting elk. The elk continued grazing, even after the grizzly was clearly in view. The bear stopped, probably puzzled at this imperturbable ungulate. After studying the elk from a short distance for a moment, the bear wandered away (maybe thinking, "Gee, I could have sworn that was dinner"). This sort of thing helps explain why it is vitally important not to run from a bear, as running seems a most promising invitation to dine.

I don't recommend charging or bluffing grizzly bears, or even ignoring them. I find the whole thing delightfully confusing.

An essential part of the expert advice, proven over time, is that if we are confronted by a grizzly bear and cannot escape by climbing a tree, we should play dead. The advice I've heard most often is that we shouldn't just roll up in a ball. We should lie flat, face down with our fingers locked behind the back of our neck and our legs spread to make it difficult for the bear to roll us over. Be still. Notwithstanding what I've already said about the unlikelihood of divine intervention, praying to the supreme being of your choice surely can't hurt.

It seems that the most damaging grizzly-hiker encounters (again, statistically speaking; there are always exceptions) are unexpected, as when a hiker surprises a bear on a kill or with a mate or young. In those circumstances the bear's nearly reflexive response is a quick defense, and a grizzly's defense puts most good offenses to shame. The idea behind playing dead is that an inert reclining being is not threatening. Though not a sure thing, playing dead has statistically proven itself the choice most likely to keep you alive.

And here's another little complication that's worth your hearing about. Longtime Yellowstone grizzly bear researcher Steve French first got interested in the bears while working as a physician treating people with serious bear injuries. Based in part on what he learned from those victims, he told me that if you've been attacked or have successfully played dead, and the bear has moved off, wait a *long* time before moving. As he explained it, a threatened bear is often concerned only with eliminating the perceived threat. If, for example, you have sustained minor injuries in the initial encounter but have assumed an unthreatening position, that may well satisfy the bear. But Steve said that at that point the bear won't necessarily go far away. You may think it's gone, but it may hang around off at a little distance, during which time it is watching you. If you start moving around too soon, the bear may come back and make a more determined effort to "eliminate the threat." Steve, drawing on handy medical terminology, likened the results of the initial attack to "outpatient" injuries, but said that

5. and **6.** Modern Yellowstone bear jams: a bear, some people, lots of expensive cameras and optics, and not a Twinkie in sight. Photos by author.

the second round of injuries are likely to be far more serious. The lesson of Steve's inquiries is that you need to be still for a lot longer time—I don't know how exactly long that may be; nor may the bear, until it happens—than you might think. Just something else to think about out there on the trail, right?

What has always puzzled me about the effectiveness of playing dead as a way to avoid serious injury is that grizzlies eat *lots* of dead bodies, feeding heavily on winter-killed elk in those springs when carrion is available. How is it that *this* "dead body," a frightened hiker, doesn't get the same treatment? Is it that though we may smell bad, we don't smell like an elk, or a ground squirrel, or any other creature the bear is used to eating? If that's the case, then we have more reason than we ever knew to be grateful for the bear's legendarily sophisticated sense of smell—a sense we've celebrated out of all reason for centuries just for the fun of it. Maybe part of the answer is that at the moment of the encounter the bear wasn't looking for carrion, though if that's what's going on I'd hate even more to be in that particular hiker's shoes in early spring, when elk carcasses are most available and bears are actively seeking them out.

On the other hand—and pay close attention here because this hand is a long way from the first hand, and it's a really big hand— there's considerable evidence that playing dead might not always be the best approach to take with an aggressive black bear. Black bears are not as frequently reported as predators on humans as grizzly bears, but such attacks do happen, and the argument has been made that you may be better off fighting back in such a case than playing dead. Steve Herrero describes instances where people have grabbed whatever "weapon" was handy—rock, branch, whatever—and went at it with a black bear that was clearly determined to hurt, kill, or eat them. I'm not making a firm recommendation here; my time on wilderness trails is quite unambitious any more, and as I've said before, we're still learning about bears. Do your homework, talk to the local experts, and keep being careful.

About the time I was helping to monitor the Gardiner dump bears, a six-hundred-pound grizzly bear, a nearly black boar, was being held for helicopter relocation at the Fire Cache at park headquarters. His culvert trap was parked in one of the long garage stalls. It was a cool dark tunnel, away from the prying eyes of tourists and most employees, a quiet and rather dank spot that I imagined might even be to the bear's liking were he not caged up in the trap.

I shuffled self-consciously the length of the passageway to the culvert at the far end and took a seat on an upended bucket about a yard from the metal grill at the front end of the trap, the end the bear faced.

There was enough light from small high windows to see him well. He was resting on his belly, his paws drawn up near his chin, his nose a few inches behind the grill. He didn't move as I seated myself, or during the fifteen or so minutes that we sat staring at each other in that damp corner.

Bears don't have big eyes, so they are lost in that infinity of fur and fat and ripplingly smooth motion, two small dark sparks evolved to deal primarily in the nearby because what else need a six-hundred-pound grizzly bear worry about? Like the Union officer who threw the auxiliary sails overboard shortly after his huge ironclad battleship was launched because nobody was going to make *him* hurry, this bear needed better eyes nowhere near so much as his neighbors did. If I'm too far away for him to see me, it's my responsibility to keep it that way. I try to look him over, but I keep coming back to the eyes. I have big hands, and his claws seem as big as my fingers; I am darkly amused that he could probably hook his claws into the grate that separates us and rip it from its welded frame. In this case, what the bear doesn't know won't hurt me.

But from the claws, I am again drawn back to the eyes, steady, unblinking, either dull beyond my comprehension or perceptive beyond my imagination, staring with evident but unlikely calm back at me. His ears are reduced by the bulk of their surroundings—a massive round skull over heavily muscled jaws—to unimportance, like some anatomical afterthought stapled indecisively to the finished animal after it left the factory. Bears hear well, but, as with their eyesight, from my bucket in front of this one I figure that they don't really need to.

When I'm not held accountable to human reason or scholarly accuracy, which is to say when I'm alone, I lapse into a rather personal approach to what interests me: I talk to things, trying to calm a squirming trout as I struggle to free a hook and release it; reasoning vainly with a horse that is more interested in trail-side clover than in getting to the corral by dark (then cussing him as I rein him in); or greeting the elk, bedded in the snow by my door, with a mixture of joy, respect, and fear. So I want to talk to this bear. I sit there wanting to *understand*, wanting to see something in those eyes besides my reflection (and not being seduced by the rhetorical opportunities of seeing oneself reflected in grizzly eyes), something in his passive stillness besides brute patience. But I don't know how to start. What to say? I know that the trout doesn't understand my reassurances, I know the horse recognizes impatience in my voice and figures he can get one more mouthful of clover before the reins pull him away, and I never have figured out what those elk think of my silly greetings, but the talking is useful, at least for me. It's a kind of reaching out.

But the bear is too much. I would ask questions if I thought the bear had answers, or if I thought that by asking them, out loud, I might sense an answer of my own. I most feel a need to express regret or apology for the circumstances of our meeting, to apologize for the idiot who baited the bear into a settled area where he had to be trapped before someone was hurt; again the bear would have no answer. I would express admiration for his size and power, or for his wildness . . . admiration, at last, for his utter independence of my admiration, or of anything else I think or want.

That is probably why he is so important to me: it's a one-way street of fascination, I caring most for his detachment and nearly alien disregard for me, caring that he can exist without caring about me. This bear is at my mercy, vulnerable to the moronic growth of commerce, the mindless pressures of human population, and the mechanical finality of a good rifle, and he doesn't even know it. He'll die someday, and all like him, never having grasped where he stood in relation to humans, never having sat on a bucket and studied one.

This is good, I decide, and it's also a little spooky. The bear in the trap suddenly seems a lot farther away, not just a yard but uncrossable distances, and I am chilled and uncomfortable on my bucket in the presence of so untouchable a spirit. I must stir uneasily, for suddenly the audience is over. From somewhere deep in the cavernous innards of the bear, like a train still far away in a mountain tunnel, a rumbling hum begins. Impatience. The menace in the sound is palpable, though the actual animal, eyes unblinking, claws at rest on the culvert floor, has not moved at all. I still can't talk to the bear, not even an "Okay, okay, I'm going," as I right the bucket, return it to its place by the wall, and with one last wistful look at those incredible eyes, hurry from the building and into the bright morning sun.

3

Arts and Craps

We love bear stories about meetings. I was hiking along and suddenly there was a bear—all I'd ever imagined, more than I ever could understand. It worked its way up a distant slope; emerged from the forest edge; rose from behind a huge log; ambled up the trail toward me; or simply materialized in plain view where an instant before there had been nothing. Those moments, those encounters with this disturbingly familiar yet achingly remote animal, may always will be near the center of our bear lore.

But I spend many hours looking for bears or just wandering around in bear country for every hour I spend actually watching one. None of the time spent looking is wasted, and not merely because it is impossible for me to consider time spent outdoors wasted. What makes the search all the more valuable is knowing that every moment I am out there, I am in the presence of bears. I now search for that presence as eagerly as I search for the animals themselves. In fact, the search for bear presence has an advantage over the search for the bear, because it is conducted on so many levels.

Anywhere I walk, ride, wade, or drive in Yellowstone, I am in the presence of thousands of past generations of bears. Consummate omnivores, they were masterful foragers, and their foraging has led them over every trail, every meadow, every ridge, countless times before my arrival. Whether or not I am sharp enough to pick up the traces, I know they are there.

7. The source of all the excitement: the bear's paw, in this case that of a grizzly bear, leaves signatures all over the landscape. Courtesy of the National Park Service.

They are there in every rollable stone in sight, each with its promise of bear treats underneath: a juicy beetle, some crickets still stiff and slow in the cold morning shade, a few succulent new shoots of grass. The same bear that may practically wallow in a deer or elk carcass becomes a fine, precise diner on these dainties. I've encountered so many freshly rolled rocks over the years that I no longer picture them as even vaguely stationary elements of the landscape. All of them, from flat little shingles to engine-block boulders, are better seen as short-range travelers, shifting a foot or so this way, then that, then another, as the bears do their daily shopping. I enjoy imagining a fast-forwarded one-hundred-year film of a bear's landscape on which these rocks hop around like water drops on a griddle. Once in a while a rock is dislodged from a slope steep enough to send it on a longer trip, many yards down the hill. The next bear along that way will view, sniff, and handle this new feature of its shopping route with special interest.

From the realization that the bear is engaged in this kind of subtle landscape redesign, it is only a short step to other awakenings. Those long front claws that make bears so dreadful in an attack have a more important purpose: bears are great diggers. So much of what bears like to eat is underground that they have become skilled and determined treasure hunters. They snuffle out, identify, and dig for many kinds of bulbs and roots, some so small it's a wonder their metabolisms can justify the effort, but it's the steadiness of the results that makes the difference; a grizzly bear rooting around for cutworm moths on a high talus slope in the Rockies may get less than a calorie per moth, but when the moths are superabundant and the bear is slurping them up, even in little bunches, the calories quickly add up into the thousands.

It's all about keeping at it. They dig out the dried plant caches of pocket gophers and may regard the pocket gopher himself as a tasty byproduct of the work. They dig out marmot dens and ground squirrel burrows. In a single day a big bear may coarsely "till" a huge patch of meadow. The next day that same bear, its nose full of the fresh scent of a family of marmots, may move a ton of soil and rock from one spot on a slope, spreading it in a long fan down the hillside below. Imagine being a marmot while that's going on at your front door.

We used to think of beavers as the most obvious and effective ecological engineers of the wilderness, the only mammals that really reshape the land. But many animals engage in such reshaping, including bears. The beavers work in the narrow bottoms of drainages, while bears are at it everywhere. Walk a trail in grizzly country and try not to notice the weathered hillside holes where a bear has gone after some rodent, or worked loose a rock; the fresher holes may give you a chill when you notice the raw parallel claw marks along the edge of the hole (the claws sometimes come close together at their points, so don't assume that the bear was small just because the marks are in a tight row). The churning of all that soil, wherever it comes to rest, affects many other lives, from the rodents the bear was seeking to the millions of micro-organisms and dozens of plant species always on the lookout for fresh raw soil to colonize. Bears are not merely great rototillers; they are among the inadvertent gardeners of their landscapes.

Where I live, the occasional Douglas fir may live several centuries, but most of the trees don't last that long. And when they die, one of the many things that may hasten their decay is the bear, astride the fallen trunk, those powerful shoulders hunched and straining as the claws pull long furrows into the wood's prospering insect communities.

But it is while they are still alive that our trees give us the most enjoyable opportunity to know bear presence. Bear folklore has few more cherished notions than the "bear tree," a sort of ursine signpost and bulletin board, which bears use in a variety of ways—chewing and rubbing being the two that naturalists have most noticed—to signify something, if not several somethings; just what it signifies has been debated by naturalists for many years.

Certainly one of the most charming if still problematic theories has been that each bear tries to bite or scratch the tree as high up the trunk as possible, to show the others that it is the largest bear around. Some old-time writers even claimed that bears would cheat by standing on a log or a rock so they could reach higher and leave the impression of greater size to the next bear who came along and saw the mark. In *The Biography of a Grizzly* (see chapter 19 for more on this book and its author), a classic of nature fiction first published in book form in 1899, the famous American naturalist Ernest Thompson Seton portrayed a sly grizzly bear doing just this in order to scare a larger bear with which he fearfully shared his home country. Though rightly remembered as a great naturalist, Seton's tendencies to anthropomorphism were often cause for comment, and in this and other ways he did perhaps err on the side of humanizing his grizzly bears a tad incautiously. But I agree with ecologist Charles Preston, who says that *Biography of a Grizzly* is still a "largely plausible glimpse into the life of a grizzly bear." It's always been hard to sort out what all might be going on in a bear's head, and the more they're studied, the more

8. and 9. Aptly termed "bear art," the aging claw marks of climbing black bears on aspen bark take many forms, depending upon each bear's size, strength, and behavior. Photos by author.

like us they become. Seton is turning out to be more right about them than his critics ever imagined.

In his book *Out on a Limb: What Black Bears Taught Me about Intelligence and Intuition*, New Hampshire biologist Benjamin Kilham has brought a discerning naturalist's gifted eye to the matter of bear "sign" and delighted many of us with his findings. I suppose that it has been our human reliance on sight more than other senses that has made generations of bear observers presume that the clues the bear reads in bear sign are primarily visual as well. Oddly, we do this despite a great deal of ancient lore across many cultures that celebrated the bear's sense of smell. Kilham—in one of those wonderful intuitive leaps that leads the rest of us to a lot of forehead slapping ("Of course! How could I have missed that?")— reminds us to pay more attention not only to our bear lore but also to what's really going on when a bear bites, scratches, or rubs a tree, walks a trail, drops a fresh load, sniffs a leaf (or another bear), or in any other way interacts with its environment: "Just as bears leave an unintentional scent trail wherever they go, they also leave distinctly intentional olfactory communications. With sebaceous oil, sweat, urine, semen, and vaginal excretions, bears deposit scent marks to manage their world and reflect their position in society—not unlike human graffiti carved into trees or painted on subway trains, rocks, or bridges."

It also appears that bears don't use only the scents they generate themselves; the scratching or biting of the tree may release the scent of the tree's own sap and resin, sending yet other meaningful messages to neighborhood bears.

Much more frequently observed bear-tree behavior involves the bear standing up against the tree trunk for a good back rub. It's been common knowledge (not that common knowledge is always, well, real knowledge) for a long time that bear trees were in some sense "signposts," but Kilham has diagnosed the effect of this behavior for us: "If you separate the hairs on a bear's back, you will likely see a concentration of oils that have built up from the many sebaceous glands found in them. When a bear does a full back rub on a tree, it is the scent these oils carry that will create its mark—and bears appear to go to great lengths to make sure as much of that oil ends up on the tree as possible."

Back in chapter 1, and later, in chapter 6, I give examples of how successful a bear can be at multimedia presentations—both sight and scent—when it signals us with a turd or two. In his book, Kilham provides many other examples of the ways in which bears make full use of the various communicative scents they generate, whether for friendly purposes ("Hey, baby!"), with hostile intent ("You lookin' at me?"), or for any of the other social possibilities that are such a routine part of bear life.

Bear lore in many parts of the world is full of tales of habitually used trails where generations of bears have walked the same path so frequently as to leave either a single path or a pair of parallel trenches or ruts. There's nothing particularly unusual about various species of wild animals, large or small, creating such paths, and they're easy enough to find in Yellowstone, especially on a bare hillside where bison or elk have created regular sidehill trails by their habitual use of the same route. Reliable bear lore takes it a step—sorry, didn't intend that pun—further, and describes places where the bears have all put their feet down in more or less the same spot, creating a dual track of parallel rows of foot-size indentations. I've seen photographs and artistic portrayals of the "double-rutted trail" of bears, perhaps first in Olaus Murie's wonderful *A Field Guide to Animal Tracks*, but I've not seen an example with the parallel sets of foot indentations in the park, though I wouldn't be surprised if others have, especially back in the days when many bears gathered at park dumps.

In the mid-1970s, a few years after the Trout Creek dump in central Hayden Valley was shut down and the many bears that fed there had either redistributed themselves out among Yellowstone's summer food buffet or found their way into fatal trouble in some developed area in or near the park, fellow ranger-naturalists Butch Bach and Don Arceneaux and I hiked into Hayden Valley. The Trout Creek dump site—Grizzly Bear Central back in the bear-feeding era—was the first stop on a day that found us meandering clear to the back of the valley, cautiously skirting a couple of randy bison herds in the midst of their rut. What I remember most about the dump site was the several uneven bear paths that extended out from the dump site toward the far corners of the valley. I don't know how long they lasted after that, and I suppose they gradually faded out the way such things do, but even in the early 1980s there was at least one bear that was known to return to dig around a little, presumably just to make sure the garbage bonanza was really over. Bears don't forget.

Next to actual tracks, I suppose that what I have spent the most time looking for is what ecologists Charles Jonkel and Jim Halfpenny have both aptly described as "bear art": the marks bears leave behind when they climb a tree. Here in the Northern Rockies, our best local tree for showing this is the aspen; its soft white bark is easily punctured and forms beautiful black scars wherever branches have fallen, or birds have poked through, or bears have climbed. It has become my favorite reminder of the neighborhood bears, because once they have climbed the tree, their "art" is there as long as the tree lasts.

Aspens are a tiny minority of our local trees, so they don't begin to reflect the number of times bears have climbed trees of other species, but they're the easiest to read so I always watch for them. Sometimes it seems that there is hardly an aspen grove in the wilder country around here that doesn't have at least one tree with claw marks from the base to thirty feet up. Some extend to the more spindly high trunk. One winter a short snowshoe hike of half a mile near Mammoth Hot Springs turned up half a dozen of these trees, each with its own unique set of signatures.

They all beg to have their story told. Was this a drama of a bigger bear, perhaps a grizzly, chasing a smaller one, and the smaller one taking refuge in the tree? Often the claw marks are not four or five neat black dots, but are instead a parallel set of curving lines, the bear having slipped a few inches or even a foot in its haste. In his splendid book *Yellowstone Bears in the Wild*, master tracker Jim Halfpenny says that the longer marks are usually made as the bear slides down the trunk. I've never heard of Jim being wrong about anything like this, so there you have it.

There is one tree near a road I often drive, a tree whose whole trunk is pocked with hundreds of claw marks, as if one day all the bears for twenty miles around decided to do their equivalent of stuffing students in a phone booth. What happened here? Was it just a sow with three or four very active cubs? Being so close to the road, I tend to assume that people were involved in some way, probably a camera-pointing crowd of them making the mother bear nervous enough to shoo her cubs up the trunk until things calmed down. But it's hard for me to tell, at least from a casual glance, if most of these marks were made fifty years ago or five.

For a sense of today's bears, the ones I might characterize as current events, I look for the newest marks. This search begins in early spring, when the first of the grizzly bears—the big males— roust themselves from their dens and go in search of food and mates. For some years in the late 1980s and well into the 1990s, the road up the north side of Mount Washburn, which overlooked the Antelope Creek drainage to the east, was perhaps the Yellowstone bear watcher's foremost hot spot. Cars and trucks of the dedicated watchers crowded at awkward angles into the informal unpaved wide spots at places along the road where the slope was gentle enough to allow for a car to perch on the edge of the drop without sliding off or obstructing traffic.

One day, shortly after that stretch of road was plowed well enough to be opened to cars, I was up there with my scope scanning the slopes, most of which were still deep in snow. It's a lot of country to see at once, many square miles of mixed forest and meadow with lots of cozy little draws and gullies inviting telescopic investigation. A bear might come into view anywhere from at the foot of the slope you're on to four or five miles off at the lip of some sharp cliff face. Once in a great while a bear might come over the ridge behind you, though I was lucky enough never to experience that particular excitement.

On this morning, there were no bears and precious few other animals in view, but pretty quickly I had as rewarding a sighting—a long deep trench in the deep snow of a high ridge a mile or so off. A big bear had, for reasons only it knew, decided it needed to

10. All the news you need to know, freshly delivered by a large Alaskan brown bear. Photo by author.

shoulder its way through that very deep, unbroken snow up from the valley and over that ridge which, I suppose, must have topped out at eight thousand or so feet.

Scenes like this broaden one's idea of the bear. Many years ago, at my most fit, I might have thought of trying to plow and push my way for a hundred yards or so through such hard, deep snow over flat terrain, but not on a ferociously steep slope like that. There are few things a grizzly bear does that can leave me with such an impression of its irresistibility as those broad, deep ditches in dense snow in which I could hardly budge.

A little later that morning, as I drove back down the road toward Tower Junction, I saw Marilynn and Steve French at their truck in one of the lower overlooks, so I pulled over to chat. As I got out of my car and walked toward Steve I could see that he had the same happy grin I did, and it was only by a matter of a second or so that he first spoke the words I was about to speak: "Did you see that trail?" It's a satisfying moment when two people, both rea-

11. and 12. Yellowstone grizzly bear piles. Photos by Jim Peaco. Courtesy of the National Park Service.

sonably practiced and tuned to the same wonders in a huge land-scape, even though a mile apart, can know that they have zeroed in on the same single telling feature of it all as what matters most.

After the snow is gone and the ground dries and hardens, find-ing tracks is more fortuitous, usually the result of poking around in streambeds where a bear stepped in soft mud. Then, though I keep looking for tracks, I know I'm more likely to come upon scat. Call it droppings, turds, crap, shit, feces, dung, or just poop, bear scat is one of the great attention getters of the wilderness. A quick examination will tell you many things about the bear: what it was eating (grabbing a handy stick, we dissect scat the way junior high biology students disassemble frogs and cats, except we're a lot more interested in what we find); how long ago it was here (even if the scat is old and dry, you shouldn't necessarily assume that its point of origin is far away); and how big it is (as I've said before, there are at times a rough correlation between diameter of scat and diameter of bear).

I have come upon big piles of soft, runny berry scat so new that they were still settling, and the juices were just beginning to run across the trail. They reminded me of the extent to which I was rou-tinely in the presence of bears; this was no abstraction. The bears were probably close to me much more often than I cared to know.

One wet spring day in Glacier National Park, Steve Gniadek, a National Park Service biologist friend, and I hiked over Stony Indian Pass, just then well known to have a lot of bear activity, both grizzly and black. We made noise constantly, not wanting to surprise, well, *anybody* at close range, and we were apparently suc-cessful enough at it that we saw no bears the whole day. But never, even when I have seen bears, have I been as aware of being in their presence as I was on that day. In the course of about five miles of trail, we passed countless diggings and saw the tracks of at least four different bears, two blacks and two grizzlies. Fairly far down the east side, we came upon a set of grizzly tracks in the muddy trail. Steve bent over for a closer look, but he abruptly straight-ened up and scanned the slopes in all directions. It took a second for me to realize that he did that because the tracks were so fresh

13. Grizzly bear tracks are generally distinguished by the prominent claw marks out front. Photo by Jim Peaco. Courtesy of the National Park Service.

that there was just no question that they had been full of bear feet just moments before. At a time like that, as much as you'd like to know where the bear is, it hardly matters that you didn't see it. Indeed, it's almost a better story without seeing it.

Thanks to our science, our technology, and our incurable curiosity, we have tracked bears into unbelievably remote corners of our often-overlapping evolutionary histories. In caves throughout Europe, paleontologists have found, besides the bones of countless bears—especially the now long-extinct cave bears—bear tracks and claw marks made in ancient muds that have since hardened and lasted all this time. But they've found something else, something that, for me at least, has a nearly chilling immediacy when I think of the many ways we experience bears. In *The Cave Bear Story*, the Finnish paleontologist Björn Kurtén described a wondrously different kind of track, the *Bärenschliffe*:

The so-called *Bärenschliffe* tell a very different story. They are found in narrow passages, on the ceiling or the walls, and sometimes on loose slabs that are now found imbedded in the cave earth but which once formed part of the ceiling or wall. They are surfaces polished to a mirrorlike sheen by the passage of innumerable bears during hundreds or thousands of years. Few things speak more eloquently of the vastness of geological time and the cumulative numbers of living beings that have trodden one and the same path than these bear-polished limestones.

I agree. Even discovering bear tracks so fresh that their edges are still crumbling, or a pile of bear crap so new that it is still settling—though such discoveries have a vital, even dire urgency right at that moment—aren't likely later to haunt the mind quite as much as will the idea of a stone polished by the gently rubbing passage of a thousand bears over thousands of years.

Part of the fulfillment of being in bear country is sustaining and even reveling in the awareness that something monumentally important is near but not visible—and is more aware of you than you are of it. Seeing the bear is a great thing, a singular opportunity for wonder, but it is also the ending of another part of the bear-country experience—accepting that most of the time you will know the bear only through the many other signs it leaves to tell you that you're not alone, so you'd better pay attention.

4

Nervous Neighbors

I t's surprising how little it takes to make a grizzly bear nervous. You'd think an animal like that would be imperturbable. But then, nervousness has always worked really well for them. In a way, nervousness helped create them.

In the mid-1990s, Steve French and I spent parts of two late-fall days on the Blacktail Plateau in northern Yellowstone National Park watching a grizzly bear guard a bison carcass. The bear was a four-and-a-half-year-old male, still young but more than big enough to impress any observer. I suppose he weighed two hundred and fifty or so pounds.

Steve and I had a good observation position, slightly higher than the bear and a few hundred yards distant, where we were no big disturbance to him. I assume that he knew we were there, but we were quiet and we didn't move around, so we just didn't matter much to him. The carcass lay at the edge of a small aspen grove with a steeper hill just beyond. Two or three little draws led up the hill from the grove into a dense pine forest.

Steve had been monitoring this carcass for a few days—it was just off one of the park's unpaved secondary roads, already closed to tourist traffic because the autumn rains made it too slippery for the average sedan driver—and had seen a variety of scavengers on it, including a black bear. The first day I went with him I happened to have the carcass in view before he did, and I said something like, "Doesn't look like a black bear today, Steve."

Grizzly bears are as fond of bison meat as are most other scavengers, but by virtue of their size they can simply take over the carcass and chase off all other interested parties (for taking a carcass from the predator or predators who killed the animal in the first place, there is a term so delightful I must italicize it for best effect: *kleptoparasitism*). They then begin to display what I call, for lack of a better term, nervousness.

Thanks to the usual effects of a harsh climate, to the normal aging processes of all animals, and to the bears, wolves, mountain lions, coyotes, and occasionally even the smaller predators, carcasses are common in Yellowstone, and are magnets for many appetites. Around any carcass more than a day or two old you can assume you'll see evidence of ravens, magpies, and coyotes, and you look with particular concern for the tracks of bears. Any time you're in bear country and you think you see a dead animal, don't just amble on up for a closer look; you don't know who's taking a nap behind it, or nearby. Bears will go to great lengths to defend a carcass, including burying it.

Burial is an intriguing behavior. Some bears will dig at least a shallow hole, roll the carcass into it, then cover it over with earth. In the 1970s, there was a grizzly bear in Yellowstone known among the researchers as Square Bear because he was observed digging a hole that actually seemed to have corners, like a grave; who knows what that was about? Other bears just pile dirt on top of the carcass until it seems like enough. In either case, large portions of the carcass may be exposed, perhaps a leg or shoulder sticking up through the dirt—burial doesn't always equate precisely with anything approaching visual concealment.

Burial seems to have more than one purpose, but I don't know what various evolutionary imperatives may be behind the behavior. I suppose that sometimes it is most effective in at least partly smothering the scent and thus making the carcass a little less easily locatable by other scavengers, though this obviously doesn't work for the ravens and magpies, who seem to show up in a matter of minutes. On the other hand, the bear digs up so much earth that the whole area around the carcass looks more like a very shallow bomb crater than a place where someone is trying to camouflage something. Such sites must often be easy to see from a long distance, or from the air, which probably helps explain the uncannily quick arrival of the birds.

Burial may also be a kind of warning sign, vaguely but not exactly like scent marking is for dogs—"This is mine, stay away." Whatever the purpose or purposes of such behavior by each individual bear, obviously the burying urge is deeply rooted.

It was certainly well rooted in this young grizzly. By the time we arrived, when he probably had only been in possession of the carcass for a day or so, there was a shallow "moat" (Steve's term) around the carcass, and piles of dirt over much of it. The grizzly had dug no hole, so the higher he piled the dirt the more obvious it was that something was there, covered over with dirt.

When we got there, he was in the position he most often occupied, sprawled on his belly right on top of the pile. Once or twice during the several hours that we watched, he exhumed some portion of the carcass and worried at it, pulling off chunks of meat. But most of the time he just protected it.

He had a very active definition of protection. A few obligatory ravens were hanging around, sometimes sitting in the trees directly above him, sometimes prancing only a feet beyond the moat, always looking for their chance. He eyed them with anxiety, often turning abruptly to stare one off, or even standing and taking a step or two toward them. A coyote got the same treatment.

If the threat seemed persistent enough, the grizzly would go back to digging, sometimes stepping toward the perceived competition, then back-digging with his forepaws rearward to the carcass. Steve later told me that after a few days, when I was no longer visiting the site with him, the bear had dug the moat so deep that he was now making longer excursions out between the aspen trees. He was just digging furrows back toward the carcass, pulling more and more dirt onto the pile.

All this proprietary activity reached its most exciting point—for us, at least—when the black bear showed up. The grizzly was resting on the pile, facing more or less northeast, when Steve suddenly noticed a black bear coming down one of the draws from the heavy woods behind the grizzly. The draw emptied into the grove maybe sixty yards behind the carcass, and the black was not yet in sight of the grizzly when we first saw it.

I must explain our excitement. Interactions between major carnivores are almost continuous in the intensely compressed timelines of television nature shows, but in the wild you're lucky to see such a thing once in a great while. Since the arrival of wolves a few years after the events I'm describing here, such encounters have become more commonly observed, as wolves have occasional run-ins with all their fellow large carnivores.

But before the wolves showed up even Steve, with many seasons of bear observations, had seen relatively few interactions between the two bear species. I, with bear experience based primarily on years of reading obscure natural history and sporting literature, had read only anecdotal and often unreliable accounts of such interactions, most taking place decades earlier in the park's garbage dumps, where large concentrations of bears put all comers in uncomfortably close proximity of each other. So for both Steve and me the opportunity to watch these two rival appetites sort out their competing interests was a big deal.

I must also elaborate on the nervousness theme here. From the moment I had them both in sight, I was, with more analytical calm than I thought I possessed, also thinking about the winding and mysteriously convoluted evolutionary trail that had brought them together here. I love these long-haul evolutionary tales. Paleontologists are wonderful detectives, and their accounts of the emergence, convergence, and disappearance of species, patiently pieced together from countless globally scattered geological leftovers, give a charming looseness to their "give-or-take-a-few-million-years" conclusions.

According to the fossil record, early during the tens of millions of years that bears, or at least bearish mammals, have existed, animals appeared that could be uneasily described as bear-dogs, or just as uneasily, as dog-bears. These were "bearesque" carnivorous mammals whose dentition, characterized by larger, flatter grinding surfaces better suited to vegetation, distinguished them

14. The North American black bear: shy by evolutionary consequence, but don't press your luck. Photo by author.

as the start of yet another of nature's headlong excursions into omnivory. It was an excursion that would result in a host of bear characters, many of whom shambled onto the evolutionary stage, looked around for a few thousand centuries, then either became someone else or just winked out altogether. The process continues on its merry and unpredictable way today, though in most parts of the world we humans, rather than the usual array of other varying environmental factors, tend to drive whatever evolutionary direction the bears will next take—assuming that we even give them enough generations to go somewhere new, evolutionarily speaking, before wiping them out completely.

But the fossil record is no longer our only archive of bear genealogy. It's not even the one most in favor with a host of researchers who are trying more accurately to trace bear lineage through the tangle of ancient ursine *begats* that led, among many other wonderful things, to the two superficially similar and yet fundamentally quite different animals that Steve and I were privileged to watch in action that day.

It is at the same time exciting and disappointing for me to admit that in just the fifty years that I have been passionately reading and thinking about bears, our scientific study of their lives has gone from a largely understandable body of research findings and folklore to a far more sophisticated sort of scholarship that, I confess, is now beyond my layman's ken. Modern molecular techniques for unraveling the evolutionary history of bears and, no doubt, many other animals I've not spent so much time reading about, are a new world of informational forms. This is a wondrous literature— filled with talk of genome analysis, phylogenetic incongruence, mitochondrial phylogeny, coalescent species trees, D-FOIL statistics, pairwise Markovian coalescent analyses, bootstrap replicates, variant call format files, and all the rest of an entire terminological universe whose structures and meanings are beyond my experience, my training, and, I fear, my aging capacity for learning. No matter how much I love the way all these terms sing right off the page at me, and no matter how eager I still am to wade through the conclusions their users reach, it seems I sometimes only enjoy them for their sound and not their meaning. I must assume that I will never to catch up with this whole branch of bear science. In this one respect the magic of the bear's world has deserted me.

That being said, it remains my great good fortune that much if not most of the bear's world is still susceptible to a determined generalist's eye and brain, and there is still abundant room for good old natural history, which has plenty to offer the semiretired amateur student of that world. In its fundamentals at least, the story of how these two bears got to Blacktail Plateau remains susceptible to the theorizing of traditional naturalists.

My friend Steve Herrero, to whom this book is half dedicated and whose lifelong study of bears is the subject of chapter 10, has long offered persuasive theories to explain the differences between black and grizzly bears. As he summarizes it, "The black bear is primarily a forest-adapted animal with something as fundamental as safety tied to the presence of its primary escape terrain, which is trees. No wonder the black bear ventures from the forest reluctantly." Shaped by its chosen escape terrain, the modern black bear (*Ursus americanus*), has short, well-curved claws most useful in tree-climbing. Black bear sows protect their cubs by sending them up trees, and if the danger is grave enough they will follow them to safety. Black bears made it to North America across the Bering Land Bridge and down into the present United States and Mexico, a few hundred thousand years ago (give or take).

The modern grizzly bear (*Ursus arctos*) became what it is by adjusting to new habitats as the Asian landscape of its ancestors changed around them. Again, here's Steve:

> I suggest that grizzly bears evolved from forest-dwelling ancestors by developing adaptations that allowed them to feed and survive in the open environments created by glacial retreat. I have described how natural selection favored longer claws and greater development of muscles related to digging for food. Natural selection also favored females that could effectively defend their cubs in a treeless environment. Here the cubs could not provide for their own protection by climbing out of harm's way. The female had to repel potential predators, and these certainly existed. Wolves were numerous, and large cats, such as the saber-toothed, were present. Other bears were threats as well, and the cubs lacked the safety of trees.

In this perilous landscape, with these mighty evolutionary forces at play, time strongly "favored aggressive female grizzly bears."

So it happened that out there at large on vast open ground, the grizzly bear's ancestors, not being able to send their cubs up a tree to safety, developed more assertive, often explosive, ways of defending them. Shaped by a very different terrain than the one that gave us the black bear, the grizzly became what we see it to be today: big, strong, disinclined by circumstances to back off, and, at least when hard put to it, quite willing to stand up to if not take a good whack at anybody who seems to pose a threat to its personal preferences of the moment.

A younger species than the black bear, grizzly bears crossed the Bering Land Bridge perhaps fifty thousand years ago (give or take) but were prevented by continental ice from reaching what is now the United States until the most recent retreat of the gla-

15. The North American grizzly bear: peaceable enough by personal preference but explosively assertive when surprised or otherwise bothered past its patience. Photo by author.

ciers about twelve thousand years ago (the gives and takes do get smaller the closer we get to the present).

All of this history has obvious and important behavioral consequences for the divergence of the black and grizzly bear species generally, and for the two bears that Steve and I were watching that day on the Blacktail Plateau. As grizzly bears adapted to the open tundra without the shelter and security of trees, their defense of cubs, mates, and food sources became, well, offensive. If you are a mother grizzly bear out in open country with no trees up which to send your cubs, or if you are a male grizzly with a mate or a fresh carcass to defend, a little nervousness is just part of your day. If you are the genetic product of tens of thousands of years of grizzly bears who survived by being good at the forceful exercising of their nervousness, you're likely to be pretty good at it yourself.

As Steve and I watched the black bear work its way down the draw, I got my first chance to compare these two species in real life, as opposed to in memories, artwork, and photographs, in which they were usually far apart. Telling the two bear species from each other is an important matter in bear country, and I had more than once written or explained that it was especially hard when only one was in view. I'm sure many national park visitors, from Yellowstone to Alaska, have gone home convinced they've seen a grizzly bear when they saw a brown-colored black bear. Far too often hunters have made the same mistake and shot a grizzly.

There was no serious comparison this time. The black bear was an adult of unknown sex, about the same weight as the grizzly, possibly a little less. It was dark brown, and though it had all the general traits of bearishness—full deep belly, heavily muscled limbs, and the like—it was immediately recognizable as anything but a grizzly. The grizzly, with its more massive head, its pronounced shoulder hump, and its brindled coat of no describable single color, had a bearing and presence nothing like the black's.

The black bear obviously knew the carcass was there and was on its way in to check it out. Steve said this wasn't the one he'd seen a few days before, which made us wonder just how many bears were involved in this picnic. When the black bear left the draw, it saw the grizzly bear and stopped to consider this dismaying development.

The grizzly, spread-eagled comfortably on its carcass pile, was in the habit of regularly lifting its snout to the wind, just to smell what might be new, but it took it a while to sense the black. In the meantime, the black, clearly disappointed at the presence of the other bear, began to feed—or pretend to do so—on vegetation along the hillside.

When the grizzly did realize the black was nearby, it reached new heights of agitation. In two days, we watched it significantly react to the apparent threat of the black bear four times, and each time do so a little differently. For starters it might dig, it might pace, it might go to a nearby tree and stand against it, scratching its back on the bark. But each time, eventually some threshold of turfy tension was crossed and it would make a quick run at the black bear.

Here I must pause to emphasize a point that I can't repeat often enough. Unless you're headed for a secure shelter or nice tall tree that is a great deal closer to you than it is to the bear, don't ever try to outrun a bear. I know they look ponderous, even when they're underway, but they can lope faster than you can sprint. The grizzly, once he decided he'd had enough of this interloper poking around in the grove, would suddenly break into a gallop—though I'm sure it wasn't his top speed—and cover the distance almost as fast as the black bear was able to reach the nearest aspen and scramble noisily twenty or thirty feet up.

There was never any question of who was dominant. The black fled the instant the grizzly charged and, once safely perched on a stout branch well up in a tree, watched the grizzly finish its charge and then wander back to the carcass. The outcome of each charge was so certain that even before the grizzly had reached the tree, he would merely be jogging along, as if tagging the trunk were just part of this little ritual of dominance. He would reach the tree, lift his front paws onto it, not fully standing upright, then turn away. By the time his paws touched it, his head had already turned. Only once did he even bother to give the black bear a nasty glare. Once he even turned his back to the tree and had a little back rub on the trunk (see chapter 3 for what this little gesture probably meant), sure beyond any question that the black bear would not take advantage and jump him from above. Then he stalked off with what I don't think I was imagining as an "I'm bad" gait, to resume his carcass sprawling.

The black would wait a few minutes, eyeing the grizzly through the intervening branches, then scoot quickly down the tree (bears can also climb up and down a tree a lot faster than you can). Both days, its first descent soon brought a second charge from the keyed-up grizzly, followed by a second treeing, and then the black was allowed to leave.

It's not always this straightforward when the two species meet. There are a number of historic accounts, including some from Yellowstone, of black bears standing their ground against grizzlies. This day we were watching all this, it occurred to us that it would be really interesting if one of Yellowstone's largest male black bears were to show up and test the younger grizzly's determination and confidence.

That thought also begs for a short concluding digression. In the informal jargon of bear watchers, there are adult females and adult males, but there are also "big males." Once both black and grizzly bear females reach adulthood, they tend to invest their energy in cub-rearing rather than in additional growth, so they more or less stop growing. But males have many reasons for wanting to get bigger and bigger, including their need to be able to win a female and keep her long enough to mate.

Incidentally, one intriguing possible outcome of this is that the bear population might wind up with a number of really large dominant males who do most of the actual mating and thus may collectively have a corner on the gene pool—and would certainly have a corner on anything else they want. Bear managers have reason for concern about this; if the bear population you're in charge of isn't all that large in the first place, and then the new cubs are being produced by only a few fathers, genetic issues relating to inbreeding could arise.

When we see one of these big guys we refer to him as a big male, though mentally I always picture the term as "Big Male" or, better yet, "Big Male, Sir." Steve told me that in all his observations of grizzly bears to that point he had yet to see a big male run, either toward or away from something. He assumed they can, of course; they just never need to. Maybe it's possible for even a grizzly bear to outgrow nervousness.

So we wondered how it would go if one of the black bear population's largest and most dominant males were to come in now and discover that this luscious carcass was in the possession of such a young and relatively inexperienced grizzly. I suspect we would have witnessed new heights of nervousness.

But it didn't happen, at least not while I was watching. My last sight of the bear that second day had him sacked out on the pile, guarding his prize. A still photograph of him would have suggested a bear dozing off, but even a moment's steady watching belied that image. His eyes might close, and he might seem to relax, but regularly, every few minutes or so, his head would come up, those bright little eyes would scan the foreground, and the nose would test the wind.

5

Almost My Favorite Bear Story

My first venture into the writing of bear books was *The Bears of Yellowstone*, published in 1980 and then twice revised, enlarged, and updated for new editions in 1986 and 1992. In the process of researching that book I discovered a nearly inexhaustible wealth of bear stories in the countless books, scientific and popular articles, diaries, official records, and other documents relating to Yellowstone. It was a great disappointment to me that I could only quote briefly from all that wonderful lore in *The Bears of Yellowstone*, so eventually I decided that it required a book of its own. I gathered up several dozen of the tastiest of these early bear-related items and published them in *Yellowstone Bear Tales* (1991), revising, expanding, and otherwise improving it for a new edition in 2013.

A couple of years after the new edition appeared, I was dismayed to discover that I'd somehow left out one of my favorite stories. The present book gives me the opportunity to get that story in print for bear enthusiasts. So here it is.

Individual tastes differing as they do, I don't claim that this little century-old tale about Bill Wade is somehow "the greatest bear story ever told," or otherwise set it up on a pedestal of supremacy. It just strikes me right. It combines a style of period humor writing I've always admired with some of the other most common elements of bear stories, including surprising circumstances, genuine peril, some laughs, and, perhaps most important, the always mystifying perspective of the bear(s) involved.

Still, recognizing that stories featuring epic bursts of profanity (no matter how vaguely described) and blasphemy (which Wade appears to indulge in clear across the spectrum of available religions, and which Freeman reports "with no consideration of its ethical bearing") are not to everyone's taste—even mine—I can only say that this piece's author, Lewis Freeman, was describing something that apparently did actually happen, and that everything he describes about the bears rings true. Besides, what I find most enjoyable about the story is the thought of that third grizzly bear, minding his own bearish business and contentedly rooting through the snow and dirt for goodies, until interrupted by an unseemly commotion, then sticking his head up out of the snow, thinking the ursine equivalent of "What the hell? . . ."

The author, journalist, and adventure writer Lewis Freeman eventually published this story in his book *Down the Yellowstone*, in 1922, but as near as I can determine, the events described probably took place about 1901, when Freeman spent some time in the park researching a story about the ruggedly heroic U.S. Army soldiers and scouts who patrolled the park in the winter to protect the wildlife from poachers.

There are a few other things you should know to comfortably read this story. One is that he chose to say "ski" whether he meant one ski or more than one. Another is that at that time many if not most people who skied in Yellowstone carried only one heavy pole, rather than the two light ones we carry today. This sturdier pole was typically used with both hands while skiing along in relatively flat country, but while going downhill the skier sometimes chose to straddle it, riding it like a witch's broom, which had the great advantage on downhill runs of allowing the skier to haul up on the stick, thus using it as a brake if needed. This was the approach taken, unsuccessfully as it turned out, by Bill Wade in the following story. One last quibble is that Giant Geyser wasn't then and isn't now "the biggest geyser in America"—though by any reasonable standard it is surely big enough.

Stories about Yellowstone bears in winter aren't all that common simply because the bears spend winters in their dens. Sto-

16. Winter in Lamar Valley. Since the park's establishment a century and a half ago, patrolling vast stretches of this snowbound wilderness has been one of Yellowstone's greatest challenges—and adventures. Photo by author.

ries about Yellowstone bears in winter one hundred years ago are much, much less common, because there were so few people around even to have a chance of such encounters. In those times, only a few people—mostly soldiers and hotel winterkeepers and their families—inhabited the park's immense high interior. The soldiers were there to watch over the wildlife, while the winterkeepers spent their time (and still do) maintaining the hotel and store buildings, which mostly meant shoveling immense amounts of snow from the roofs so the buildings wouldn't collapse under the weight. Winter tourists were essentially unheard of, and because of the insistent prevalence of a poaching culture in the surrounding communities, anyone else seen in the park after the snow fell, or before the park opened to the public again in June, was openly regarded with suspicion.

With that minimum necessary background, we are ready to join Mr. Freeman, Bill Wade, their associates, and some unanticipated new acquaintances on Yellowstone's winter trails. The story is taken from his 1922 book *Down the Yellowstone*.

This has been a memorable day, for in the course of it I have seen two of the most famous manifestations of the Yellowstone in action—the Giant Geyser erupting and Bill Wade swearing. The Giant is the biggest geyser in America, and Bill Wade is reputed to have the largest vocabulary of one-language profanity in the Northwest. True, there is said to be a chap over in the legislature at Helena that can out-cuss Wade under certain conditions, but he is college bred, speaks four languages and has to be under the influence of liquor to do consistent work. Wade requires no artificial stimulants, but he does have to get mad before he can do himself full justice. Today something happened to make him sizzling mad. The eruption of the Giant is startling and beautiful, the river, as it takes its three-hundred-foot leap to the depths of the Grand Canyon, is sublime and awe-inspiring, but for sheer fearsomeness Wade's swearing—viewed dispassionately and with no consideration of its ethical bearing—is the real wonder of the Yellowstone.

We were climbing the hill back of the Fountain Hotel—Wade, two troopers and myself. Wade, who is the winter keeper of the hotel and not too skilled with ski, tried to push straight up the steep slope. Halfway to the top he slipped, fell over a stump, gained fresh impetus and came bounding to the bottom over the hard crust, a wildly waving pin-wheel of arms, legs and clattering ski. He was torn, bruised and scratched from the brush and trees, and one of his long "hickories" was snapped at the instep. For the moment he uttered no word, but the soldiers, who knew what was coming, held their breath and waited in trembling anticipation. The air was charged as before a thunderstorm. A hush fell upon us all, a hush like the silence that settles upon a ring of tourists around Old Faithful as the boiling water, sinking back with gurgling growls, heralds the imminent eruption.

Wade removed his ski, laid the fragments on the snow and folded his coat across them, as a pious Mussulman spreads his prayer-mat. Seating himself cross-legged on the coat, he cast his eyes heavenward, on his face an expression as pure and passionless as that on the countenance of the Sistine Madonna. For a few moments he was silent, as though putting away earthly things and concentrating his mind on the business at hand. Then he began to summon the powers of heaven and the powers of hell and to call them to reckoning. He held them all accountable. Then came the saints—every illustrious one in the calendar. Saint by saint he called them and bade them witness the state they had brought him to. Spirits of light, imps of darkness—all were charged in turn.

His voice grew shriller and shriller as his pent-up fury was unleashed. He cursed snow, hills, snags, stumps, trees and ski. He cursed by the eyes, as the sailor curses, and by the female progenitor, as the cowboy. He cursed until his face turned from white to red, from red to purple, from purple to black; he cursed till the veins in knots and cords seemed bursting from his forehead; he cursed till his voice sunk from a bellow to a raucous howl, weakened to convulsive gasps and died rattling in his throat, till brain and body reeled under the strain and he sank into a quivering heap at our feet.

I shall always regret that the eruption of the Park's greatest geyser came after, rather than before, that of Wade. Frankly, the spouting of the mighty Giant seemed a bit tame after the forces we had just seen unleashed [sic] over behind the hotel.

Wade, coming through to Norris with us this afternoon, got into more trouble. Unfortunately, too, it was under conditions which made it impracticable to relieve his feelings in a swear-fest. The snow around the Fountain was nearly all gone when we started, and we found it only in patches along the road down to the Madison. After carrying our ski for a mile without being able to use them, we decided on Holt's [U.S. Army civilian scout Peter Holt] advice, to take the old wood trail over the hills. This, though rough and steep, was well covered with snow. We all took a good many tumbles in dodging trees and scrambling through brush, Wade being particularly unfortunate. Finally, however, we reached the top of the long winding hill that leads back to the main road by the Gibbon River. Here we stopped to get our wind and tighten our ski thongs for the downward plunge. At this point we discovered that the snow of the old road had been much broken and wallowed by some large animals.

"Grizzlies," pronounced Holt, as he examined the first of a long row of tracks that led off down the hill. "Do you see those claw marks? Nothing like a grizzly for nailing down his footprints. Doesn't seem to care if you do track him home."

The last words were almost lost as he disappeared, a grey streak, around the first bend. Carr and I hastened to follow, and Wade, awkwardly astride of his pole, brought up the rear. I rounded the turn at a sharp clip, cutting hard on the inside with my pole to keep the trail. Then, swinging into the straight stretch beyond, I waved my pole on high in the approved manner of real ski cracks, and gathered my breath for the downward plunge. And not until the air was beginning to whip my face and my speed was quite beyond control, did I see two great hairy beasts standing up to their shoulders in a hole in the middle of the trail. Holt was on them even as I looked. Holding his course until he all but reached the wallow, he swerved sharply to the right against the steeply sloping bank, passed the bears, and then eased back to the trail again. A few seconds later he was a twinkling shadow, flitting down the long lane of spruces in the river bottom.

The stolid brutes never moved from their tracks. I made no endeavor to stop, but, adopting Holt's tactics, managed to give a clumsy imitation of his superlatively clever avoidance of the blockade. Venturing to glance back over my shoulder as I regained the trail, I crossed the points of my ski and was thrown headlong onto the crust. Beyond filling my eyes with snow I was not hurt in the least. My ski thongs were not even broken.

My momentary glance had revealed Wade, eyes popping from his head and face purple with frantic effort, riding his pole and straining every muscle to come to a stop. But all in vain. While I struggled to get up and under way again, there came a crash and a yell from above, followed by a scuffle and a gust of snorts and snarls. When I regained my feet a few seconds later nothing was visible on the trail but the ends of two long strips of hickory. Scrambling up the side of the cut and falling over each other in their haste, went two panic stricken grizzlies.

Wade kicked out of his ski, crawled up from the hole, and was just about to spread his swear-mat and tell everything and everybody between high heaven and low hell what he thought of them for the trick they had played on him when, with a rumbling, quizzical growl, a huge hairy Jack-in-the-Box shot forth from a deep hole on the lower side of the road. Burrowing deep for succulent roots sweet with the first run of spring sap, the biggest grizzly of the lot had escaped the notice of both of us until he reared up on his haunches in an effort to learn what all the racket was about. A push with my pole quickly put me beyond reach of all possible complications. Poor Wade rolled and floundered for a hundred yards through the deep snow before stopping long enough to look back and observe that the third grizzly was beating him three-to-one—in the opposite direction. So profound was his relief that he seemed to forget all about the swear-fest. My companions claim they never knew anything of the kind to happen before.

6

Bears at the Door

By 2003, after my wife, Marsha, and I had lived more years in Yellowstone than even the luckiest people should imagine possible—including the previous nine years in one of the charming historic houses from the Fort Yellowstone era—Marsha, all at once, decided to retire. Late one afternoon she marched in the door and summarily announced that she was done, and from now on she was going to be an artist.

This was no surprise, and though I have never happily left Yellowstone even if just for an afternoon, I knew it was time. Marsha had been Chief of Public Affairs in Yellowstone for eleven years, a terribly demanding position I firmly believed no person, and especially not one as fundamentally nice as Marsha, should hold for more than three or four years. She was blessed with great bosses and had assembled a fine staff, but it was an exhausting, high-stakes, high-stress job. She was spokesperson for, and often the most visible face of, the world's most famous national park, where at least half a dozen controversies were always simmering along. The hostilities generated by such exhilaratingly beautiful things as bison, elk, grizzly bears, wildland fire, winter, and the park's other wonders were unimaginable to the millions of visitors who showed up every year for fun and inspiration in this magical place. My friend and longtime supervisor John Varley, who was himself often on the front lines in these same glorified pissing contests, was fond of pointing out to the uninitiated that Yellowstone was the only national park in the world whose heated

6

management issues could make the front page of the *New York Times* above the fold.

Thus Marsha was, in effect, Chief Park Flak-Catcher, dealing daily with a host of congressional staffers, other federal agencies, state and local officials, national and international media, special-interest groups beyond counting, and random members of the public, an unsettling number of whom were visibly crazy. If some unhinged wacko barged into the Public Affairs Office, her staff's desks featured "panic buttons" they could push so that numerous large rangers materialized within seconds.

It must be said that a great many, perhaps even most, of the people Marsha dealt with were smart and professional and were sometimes as essential to the successful running of the park as were her many colleagues in the National Park Service. But too many others, even if they weren't actually unbalanced, were what her longtime supervisor, Superintendent Bob Barbee, referred to as "self-listeners"—misguided, ignorant, greed-driven, or simply stupid people with wildly exaggerated notions of their own importance and only a feeble grasp of the park's reasons for existing. Upon hearing of her retirement plans, another friend and Yellowstone colleague of ours shook his head knowingly and said, "Yeah, of all the jobs in the park, hers is pretty much all assholes all the time."

Eleven years at the center of all that *sturm und drang* was, indeed, more than enough for anybody, but such was Marsha's sense of duty and her devotion to the mission of the National Park Service that I think she would have stuck with the job to some eventual and probably bitter end had she not discovered a passion for painting. And I'm pleased to remember that her discovery of the joys of painting was, quite by accident, something that the bears of Yellowstone and I played a part in.

In the early 1990s, when Marsha and I first got together, I was spending great amounts of time out looking for bears. I'd identified a few small but ideally situated hills not far from roads, places I could easily walk to with my spotting scope and quietly scan a great stretch of glorious wilderness where, with luck, once in a while, I could see a bear. It was never boring because there was always so much else to see while I waited.

Marsha was no stranger to bears, having spent two years living and working in Denali National Park, Alaska, prior to coming to Yellowstone. In Yellowstone, bears were one of the frequently controversial management issues she tended to, and she'd served a term as chair of the U.S. Interagency Grizzly Bear Committee's Information and Education Subcommittee, from which position she got a good look not only at bear management and bear science but at the bears themselves.

With that background, Marsha naturally thought it would be a great idea to join me on my bear-watching outings, so she started coming along. But—rather the way we call it "fishing" rather than "catching"—just because it was called bear watching didn't necessarily mean there would be a lot of bear seeing. We soon discovered that if I couldn't show her a bear—preferably a sow with a cute cub or two—in the scope's viewfinder within half an hour or so, she'd get pretty restless. This had a wonderful result, because to fill in the time she started bringing along a sketch pad. While I patiently scanned thousands of acres of wild country for any sign of a bear—or any other animate object of interest, really—Marsha would settle down to draw or paint any nearby wildflowers, or a pretty rock, or a distant ridgeline—and by all means a bear, if I obliged with one. The thrill of this art was a life-changing discovery for her.

Soon we were driving to town so she could attend art classes and workshops, where she found a kindred spirit, the gifted and celebrated artist Susan Blackwood. Under Susan's inspired mentoring, which continues to this day, Marsha's serious education in painting commenced. Many was the wild winter night we drove the eighty-some miles back to the park from Bozeman after one of Susan's classes. It seemed to us that Bozeman Pass and the Yellowstone Valley saved up its most uncooperative weather for just those nights, but it was worth every patch of black ice, every whiteout, every sudden deer looming in the headlights, every white-knuckled mile. Watching Marsha flourish as an artist was almost as exciting for me as it was for her.

So that day in 2003 when she marched into the kitchen and announced she was done, Marsha knew exactly where she would go next. We'd recently bought a small townhouse in Bozeman, thinking to retire there off in some vague and distant future, which suddenly became right now. I would continue my part-time work, as a telecommuting employee of Yellowstone National Park, and Marsha would paint.

She got a slow start. Her last months of work in the park became steadily more demanding as her retirement date approached, so by the middle of December, when the retirement parties were over, the yard sale was a happy memory that paid the movers, the house was scrubbed and cleaned, and we loaded the last bits of our stuff into our car and drove north, she was thoroughly fried. For the first two months in our new home she mostly slept, but then one late-winter day I heard her stirring around in her studio, and she was back in gear. In what seemed to me like no time at all, she was producing accomplished watercolors and having small shows at coffee shops and other local venues. On the side, now and then, she'd turn out fifteen or twenty drawings to illustrate whatever book I was writing. Eventually we reversed those roles and did a book about Glacier National Park that starred her paintings and featured my writing, which, I often commented, was just there to keep the beautiful paintings from crashing into each other.

Her art became a regular feature at our favorite coffee shop on Main Street, the Leaf and Bean, where the owner, Kate Wiggins, recognized that Marsha was not only a good artist but was also thoroughly professional about it—that apparently being a trait in short supply among many local artists. Besides Marsha's scheduled shows, I lost track of the number of times that Kate called to tell her that whatever artist who was supposed to hang a new show the next day had gone all artsy-angsty and failed to deliver. There was going to be a bare wall—could Marsha fill it? That was always great fun, as we'd immediately go around the house gathering up a dozen or so paintings among which we could identify some common theme so the show could have a meaningful title, the better to announce it in a promotional mailing and the local newspaper. First thing the next morning we'd take the pictures down to "the Bean" and hang them on those lovely, nail-ridden old brick walls, usually under the fortifying influence of Kate's mochas and scones.

We'd been living the Bozeman life this way for about three years when we realized the extent to which bears occasionally invaded our part of town. Even then, though Bozeman's suburbs were already metastasizing down the Gallatin Valley at a shocking rate, it was not uncommon to encounter large mammals right in town. Our little townhouse development is on the south side, a mile or more from the nearest forested public lands, but deer are common. My best guess is that there are enough small, narrow patches of heavy cover along the creeks and trails that meander through this older part of town that at least some of these deer are seasonal or even full-time residents who make a comfortable living grazing and browsing the neighborhood lawns and shrubbery at night. There are tracks all over the place after every snow.

Large carnivores are another matter. There have been a few worrisome reports of mountain lions on town trails over the years, but our most common carnivorous visitors are black bears (I don't doubt that right now there are grizzly bears within ten miles of our house; they just don't come to town). Back then, every fall, a few black bears would show up, apparently having made their way from the edges of Gallatin National Forest down the Sourdough Creek drainage into town. They clearly knew their way to the back yards with apple trees and other goodies, and they rarely caused any trouble other than the unsettling surprise that naturally occurred when someone ran into one unexpectedly. People were mostly careful, and the bears certainly were. Having just moved from Yellowstone's park headquarters, where we routinely had elk and bison grazing on our lawns, and where even grizzly bears were not unknown in the village now and then, we enjoyed the idea that we were still living in real bear country.

Late one evening that fall of 2006, our neighbor Sally, whose townhouse adjoined ours on the west side, called and I answered the phone.

"Hello?"

"Don't go out back! There's a big ol' brown bear on our patio right now!" Sally and Tom's bird feeders were the apparent appeal right then, though the bear didn't come over to investigate ours.

Of course, telling me not to go look at that bear was exactly the wrong thing to say, but I still regret that I somehow restrained myself and didn't rush out for a good look or a few photos.

About the same time, the newspaper reported that a bear, apparently getting confused during a nocturnal ramble down Main Street, had for some reason run head-on into a locked shop door, doing some expensive damage but then apparently not taking advantage of the broken door to explore the premises. There was, as far as we could tell, a curious and gratifying restraint among most of Bozeman's bears.

So we didn't see that one on Sally's patio, nor did we see the next one, though it made its presence known on a more personal level. One morning we looked out our French doors onto our little backyard patio and saw a small and very fresh pile of bear poop on the door mat. The same thing happened again only a few days later—the very same spot, the very same sort of little pile.

These precisely targeted piles may not have spoken volumes, but they did speak several intriguing paragraphs. As I mentioned earlier, bears don't hesitate to make a variety of statements by means of their various "traces." Just as the big male grizzly bear I mentioned in chapter 1 laid claim to the female he was following around by strategically dropping a pile directly on top of each of her piles, it was hard to imagine that this little black bear wasn't announcing something. For one thing, the bear did it twice in the very same spot. For another, this was not a casual, cutting-loose-as-I-walk-along dump; the bear had to stop whatever else it was doing and back its butt up right against the back door before unloading. The placement spoke of serious intention.

But what was intended, and what was being announced? What vitally important bearish message was being delivered? And to whom was it addressed? Had a human left such a pile in such a location, we would have a pretty good idea what was intended, but we won't get anywhere with this inquiry without first disengaging from our own species' distinctive scatological imperatives and thinking at least a little like a bear.

Turfiness of some sort comes to mind right off. Bears don't establish and defend clearly defined and bounded home ranges the way some animals do, but as we've already seen they are well known for their possessiveness of smaller realms, in the form of a female or the ground right around a fresh carcass. If the example of chapter 1's big male grizzly has any application at all here, this little black bear was staking some kind of claim to the door mat, if not to the whole backyard. This was before our townhouse association wisely if regretfully banned birdfeeders for the very reason that they did attract bears, so perhaps there were some good seed piles under our two or three feeders, though none of the feeders were themselves damaged by the bears that year. Maybe the piles were just a reminder to make sure we kept the feeders well stocked.

On another hand—and there could be several hands to consider in this sort of inquiry—I suppose the message could have been less formal or assertive, maybe more along the lines of a casually delivered Kilroy-was-here note in passing. If you have to put it somewhere anyway, why not put it to use, right? We share so many traits and behavioral quirks with bears. Why not allow them the sort of irrepressible ego that compels humans to scrawl their name on things that were doing just fine without such adornments?

Rather than take this bear's bold signature personally, or find it offensive or even threatening, we got a big kick out of it. Whatever impulse or opinion the bear was expressing, and to whatever extent it was directed at us particularly, we thought the whole thing was a hoot.

More than that, Marsha recognized this bear's "little presents" as an artistic invitation, and she was soon hard at work on a series of "Bozeman Bears" watercolors. Our daily walks routinely took us up and down the town's oldest, prettiest streets, past countless historic, lovely, or otherwise appealing locations that were themselves sources of material for local artists, and Marsha put several of those locations to work. Her painting *Sunday Stroll* featured a

17. Marsha Karle and her "Bozeman Bears" show at the Leaf and Bean coffee shop, Bozeman, Montana. Photo by author.

bear sow with two cubs lingering near the Episcopal Church on Olive Street. In *The Critics* the same bear family were window shopping at one of the Main Street art galleries (the window display showed some of Marsha's own wildlife paintings). *Joe Cool* was a slouchy juvenile bear leaning on a downtown lamp post, presumably eyeing chicks. *The Botanist* was a cub exploring a tangled bed of sweet peas (Bozeman's most famous annual event is its Sweet Pea Festival). My favorite picture was *Carnivore Club*, in which a black bear has taken a seat at the feet of "Big Mike," the extraordinary life-size replica skeleton of a *Tyrannosaurus rex* that symbolically welcomes visitors to the Museum of the Rockies, a few blocks from our house; the bear and the dinosaur are joined by a raven and two magpies—one of whom has just alighted on Mike's bony snout. But *The Gardener*, in which a black bear appears to be emerging from a tall hedge of pale red hollyhocks—those being not only one of the great American alley flowers, but a subject to which Marsha has returned frequently in her art—was a close second.

Kate was happy to hang the completed set—nine paintings, as I recall—at the Bean, where they came to the attention of a friend

18. *Carnivore Club* by Marsha Karle. Photo by author.

19. *Sunday Stroll* by Marsha Karle. Photo by author.

20. *The Critics* by Marsha Karle. Photo by author.

of ours, reporter Scott McMillion, at the *Bozeman Chronicle*. Over the years Scott had frequently worked with Marsha while covering countless Yellowstone stories for the *Chronicle*. He was also a well-credentialed bear writer himself; his *Mark of the Grizzly* was, and I assume probably still is, one of the most popular of modern western bear books. When he heard of the show, Scott interviewed Marsha and did a cover feature in the paper's weekly *This Week* supplement. *Carnivore Club* made the cover, and there was a nice center spread featuring some of the watercolors, along with Scott's interview with Marsha, in which they made the most of the opportunity to speak kindly of the bears and encourage people to be thoughtful and careful about how we all handle this slightly edgy situation.

I loved all this, not just for the validation Marsha was getting of her art but as a continuation of her good work on behalf of bears when she was in the National Park Service. And it was of course absolutely necessary for me to point out to her that even after retiring, she just couldn't seem to keep out of the papers.

There was yet another round of validation to come. One morning, just a couple days after Scott's story ran, I was busy being a part-time National Park Service employee, sitting in the front room yakking on the phone with a colleague, when I heard Marsha's phone ring upstairs. A few second later she came thundering down the stairs and stood hopping up and down in obvious excitement about something while I hastily explained to my friend that I needed to hang up. As soon as I had, Marsha burst out with, "Someone bought them all! Someone bought them all!"

From the hanging of several of Marsha's previous shows, and from conversations with some of her artist friends, I had already learned that the many joys of these local shows—perhaps the most important being the inestimable opportunity to share and celebrate the work of one's heart—did not often include a lot of sales. To have someone come in and sweep the wall clean was a delightful moment, but it was almost unheard of, too.

Thus the final treat of this little episode was that Kate's call to Marsha included the usual inquiry but with an unusual twist: your pictures all sold, but that wall's blank again—could you fill it with more pictures? And of course we could.

TWO

Bears at Home

7

Something Like Bear Hunting

About fifty years ago, the week before Thanksgiving, I went deer hunting with my brother-in-law Harry Harding in central Michigan. Harry's gone now, so it's safe to brag about him without him having to smile and say, "Aw shucks." He was a terrific outdoorsman with a seemingly intuitive grasp of everything that had to do with getting around in the forests and rivers thereabouts. He also had a reputation as a good tracker and had been getting his deer pretty much annually since childhood in these very forests. Besides how much I always enjoyed his company, anyway, it felt like an honor just to be in the woods with him, watching him exercise his skills.

I have many powerful memories from that trip, the most poignant being that right after Thanksgiving, when my sister Debbie and their kids had come up from their home near Detroit to join us for the holiday, Harry received a call that his dad had died, at which point we abandoned the north country for the long and very quiet drive back south for the funeral.

But a few days earlier, on a hunt along the edges of a huge commercial tree farm, when Harry had sent me off in a promising direction with instructions on how and where to meet up with him later, I happened to wander into a dense and uniform grove of tree-farm evergreens. It was unpleasantly cold, and I was encased in many thick layers of coats and ear-covering hat and hood, heightening the stuffy stillness of the needle-cushioned forest floor under the solid, dark canopy. All sound was muffled and diffuse, so the growls were especially alarming when they came.

Being in well-known black-bear country, Harry, his friends and relatives, and I had already had several conversations about bears, and though I was familiar with the statistically established near-harmlessness of black bears from my work in Yellowstone, the bears I'd seen in the park hadn't crept around in heavy cover growling at me like this. Momentarily ignoring good natural history—any predator trying to sneak up on me would know better than to alert me by growling—I felt stalked, and kept anxiously looking around, my .30–06 at the ready, expecting at any moment to see a gigantic *Outdoor Life*–cover-grade bear coming raging out from behind one of the nearest trees.

Finally—it was probably only a few seconds but felt like several minutes—I happened to turn in just the right way, thus twisting my various garments a bit and loosening my hood, so that I could more clearly hear the growls and identify their source in this acoustically problematic atmosphere. The gloomy stillness was suddenly broken by my embarrassed but unrestrained laughter.

The growling was coming from my stomach. Ever since arriving at his little hunting-camp cabin a few days earlier, Harry and I had been subsisting on his rudimentary bachelor-style cooking and the fare at the local Café Gutbuster. Our digestive processes bordered on the volcanic, and the noise-dissipating forest colluded with my ventriloquizing garments to throw my internal rumbles and snarls off into the vague near distance.

It's enough that I found the whole thing so entertaining, but here's a second result of this nonadventure. Even after sharing my embarrassing moment with Harry and the rest of the crew for another round of laughter, I retained a secondary and equally fine memory of it. For a little while there, I had been pretty certain that there was a big bear dangerously close to me. I was almost as certain that it was stalking me and that any minute I might be shooting at it. This is to say that, as silly as the situation turned out to be, I briefly found myself in the authentic and vividly suspenseful act of something very like bear hunting.

I don't mind telling you that there for a minute it was pretty exciting.

8

Embryonic Journeys

I n my natural history readings I have wandered among several literatures, wading determinedly through the most technical and progressively less penetrable scientific monographs, but as often slipping into that vast and troubled body of popular publication known by scientists as "the gray literature," or, less kindly, "the throwaway press." Often, the best the throwaway press has to offer is in its older forms, especially nature and sporting books and periodicals from before about 1920, back when an "outdoor magazine" might contain as much natural history lore as it did hunting and fishing stories.

I will never let go of my appreciation for this boundless source of anecdotal information on the natural world, and I have often depended upon it heavily. Early in my life, as a young writer on many natural history topics, I began to explore this sprawling, obscure, and inconveniently scattered library of lore and adventure, with both excitement and a sense of obligation. My education was, after all, in American history rather than in biology; I had much catching up to do.

This was long before the World Wide Web, back when interlibrary loan services offered a similar if much, much slower and less exhaustive role; when every source I found was mined for possible mentions of or citations to another likely source, which might lead to another source. It was a great treasure hunt, and taught me that in any historical research you can all too easily not look long or hard enough, but it's almost impossible to look too much.

It also taught me never to underestimate the smarts of generations of people who wrote on any given subject long before I did. After all, most of the questions an amateur like me might have about nature were almost certainly asked long ago by thoughtful random observers, as well as by scientists. If all I want is answers, I just read the prevailing science in the first place. But there's nothing quite like stumbling around in the dark with previous generations of question askers to teach you how we got to know what we know today.

And so it is that I rarely hesitate to invest time in old hunting, fishing, and adventure books, and in great old periodicals like *American Naturalist, Forest and Stream*, and even the venerable *American Turf Register*, whose distinguished career in pioneering American outdoor journalism ended well before the Civil War. For my purposes, the older the better. I didn't especially care what we misunderstood recently; I wanted to know how we got it wrong in the first place. I wanted to trace our natural history education from abject ignorance all the way up to modern times and enlightened, well-informed ignorance. That's how it went when I began to dig deep into the many forgotten corners of bear literature.

Within a few miles of where I'm sitting as I write this, any number of large male bears—both black and grizzly—are in the last few weeks of their winter denning. Not long after they emerge, single subadults and then females with young will also appear. I'm only one of many writers to celebrate the extraordinary evolutionary achievement of winter denning. I'm not sure that even with the amazing research work that has now been done on the subject we can ever say enough about the wonder of winter denning.

Specifically I'm talking about delayed implantation, or embryonic diapause, a scientifically well-documented phenomenon that suggests just how flexible mammalian physiology can be. Delayed implantation is a process by which a newly fertilized egg halts development at what is called the blastocyst stage, when it's just a tiny bundle of cells, and floats more or less freely in the reproductive tract of the animal for an extended period of time. After this time—whatever time works best for the animal in question—the egg implants itself in the uterine wall, resumes normal development, and the fetus then continues its growth until birth.

For a long time, probably centuries, we've struggled to come to terms with the mystery revealed by casual observations of pregnant bears. Every now and then, as I excavated bear lore from eighteenth- and nineteenth-century bear stories, I'd find some writer puzzling over the apparent conundrum that, as one early North American observer put it, "There is one thing very strange and remarkable of this Creature, which is, that no man, either *Christian* or *Indian*, ever killed a She-bear with Young."

It is precisely this kind of offhand remark, just a casual aside in some long-forgotten narrative, that speaks volumes of mystery to the alert reader. Huh? What's that? Nobody ever killed a pregnant female bear? How could that be? What are the odds that all those thousands of hunters would only kill barren or unimpregnated sows, never once finding a partially developed fetus? It's not possible.

But of course it is; that's just what happened. Or, rather, it's what all those hunters *thought* happened. And just why they thought that is a satisfying, even wondrous, example of how richly layered with questions an animal's secret biology can be.

Black and grizzly bears usually mate in late spring and early summer. But implantation is almost immediately delayed, so the blastocyst remains tiny and thus more or less invisible to human vision until November or so, when implantation occurs, just about the time the bear enters her den. Delayed implantation also gives the bear some survival options. In *Walking with Bears*, Terry DeBruyn's fascinating memoir of ten years studying black bears in Michigan's Upper Peninsula, he describes an important advantage of the delay, "Whether or not the blastocyst develops into a cub is thought to depend on the nutritional status of the female. If she does not achieve a certain body weight (or perhaps percent of body fat), or some critical physiological state, she will abort the pregnancy and reabsorb the blastocyst or give birth to nonviable offspring."

Once in the den, and assuming that her biological system has judged her condition hospitable to the rest of the pregnancy, the sow experiences a fairly short active gestation period for such a large animal, and the cubs are born in midwinter, say, late January. They weigh a pound or less at birth and grow to five or ten pounds by the time their mother leads them out of the den in April.

This explains why, lacking microscopes to examine the reproductive tracts of dead bears, and having no contact with the few scientists who even then may have had some restless notion that something like delayed implantation might be occurring in some animals, our hunter-naturalist forefathers assumed that the sows they killed and butchered were not pregnant. Evidence of the pregnancy was just too small to see.

Tracing this question and its eventual resolution through progressive ages of nature writing is an illuminating inquiry into changing perspectives and even values. Some writers just stuck with what they'd seen. Having no evidence that bears were pregnant before winter, they announced that bears must mate in the fall, presumably just before disappearing into their dens. Others, knowing that bears mated in early summer because they'd watched them doing it, simply fell silent, and probably a little glum, about the whole matter. Looking back on the larger social context of those times, I imagine that many others avoided the whole topic of bear reproduction out of Good Taste, not really wanting to deal with the sexual shenanigans of "beasts" in the first place.

We have a much better grasp of bear biology now, but let's not get smug about it. Delayed implantation is now well documented, but there are questions. When I started reading about delayed implantation, I had a few myself. Far be it from me to suggest that I could have handled this whole thing better than evolution did, but I still have to wonder how some of the choices got made.

I could see right off why it made sense for the sow to give birth to very small young. After all, she was stuck in the den, and if she gave birth to cubs that had developed through a full seven- or eight-month pregnancy, they would drink her dry of milk in a matter of days. But with the cubs born weighing only a few ounces, their milk needs were manageable, and they could continue their fetal development, so to speak, outside the womb but still within

21. "Newborn Montana grizzly cub in Central Park [zoo], New York City, Jan. 17, 1901. Length 8½ in.; weight 1½ lbs." Drawing by Ernest Thompson Seton. From Seton, *Life Histories of Northern Animals.*

the greater "womb" of the den, being essentially fully grown newborns when the family finally emerged into daylight.

But there are other questions of timing. Why not just mate in the fall and let the egg implant immediately? Well, I'm not sure, but I imagine it has to do with the need to get the very time-consuming and nutritionally draining (for the male, especially) business of mating out of the way early in the year, before the bear's metabolism goes into high gear and it begins to put on heavy fat for the coming winter. Late summer and early fall would be an inopportune time to interrupt with mating which, for a male at least, might well mean weeks of distractedly moping around near a female until she's ready to tolerate him, and perhaps having to participate in some exhausting or even damaging bashing and chomping of other male mopers who also would like to share their genes with the diffident female at issue. Those last two or three months before denning are when bears must concentrate all their energy on their annual binge of overeating, known as hyperphagia, that will build up sufficient reserves of fat to get them through the winter. It's also when some of their richest food sources are available.

That answer—that bears are too busy larding up for their winter denning—sounds acceptable, but it doesn't entirely satisfy me. The elk, deer, and bighorn sheep in my neighborhood all mate in the fall, and though it's more than some of the males can do to struggle through the winter after all that single-minded exertion, many manage to do so, and given half a chance the herds flourish under the arrangement.

On the other hand, those browsers and grazers don't den. They have to keep eating all winter, and though they don't thrive on the dried plant matter they dig out of the snow it does help slow down their weight loss and physical deterioration (I never will tire of quoting my former Yellowstone colleague Norm Bishop's characterization of the grazers' diet: "All summer they eat the cereal and all winter they eat the box"). Instead, bears completely stop eating, so every late-summer mouthful counts. Winter is a lean time, whether you spend it in a comfy den nursing hungry cubs or out on some blizzard-swept ridge trying to make a living on dead grass stems.

But on to other questions. Why not just go ahead with your usual plan to mate in early spring (if you're a bear, I mean), and your usual plan to delay implantation until fall, but *then* carry the fetus through a full-term pregnancy and give birth in spring? That way, you'd avoid the whole problem of feeding cubs in the den. Well, early spring can be a lousy time for bear food in a lot of the high places where bears live, and bears take the first few weeks to get their digestive systems into a routine of eating heavily again. I suppose that would be an awkward time to also be going through the stress of giving birth to large and very hungry cubs. Besides, I'm sure that a lot of important bonding must go on during those two months that the cubs spend in the den with their mother.

Maybe there are physiological limits to how long the bear's system can delay implantation. Maybe it's not a coincidence that implantation seems to occur just about the time denning occurs; maybe the remarkably involved metabolic processes associated with gearing all your systems (if you're a bear, I mean) for hibernation put certain limitations on what the bear's reproductive system can get away with.

Delayed implantation occurs in many mammals. A partial list includes several bats, badgers on three continents, fisher, mink (because they're raised in large numbers in captivity for furs, they've

22. Of the countless decisions a mother bear must make, some of the most important ones, such as whether or not she'll have cubs in a poor food year, are involuntarily made on her behalf by her internal biology long before the cubs are born. Photo by author.

been unusually well studied in matters like this), skunks, more than a dozen species of seal, batches of mice and rats, shrews, moles, roe deer, and the armadillo, which may hold the record, being able to delay implantation for well over a year.

What's more, they do it in many different ways. Some, like the bears, have a seasonal cycle that's pretty well fixed: spring mating, summer delayed implantation, fall implantation. Others, like some of the mice, are known to breed actively over an extended period of time, so delayed implantation seems to kick in if environmental stress alerts the animal's system that in nutritional terms it would be a bad time to develop fetuses. The female red kangaroo may carry an unimplanted blastocyst at the same time that she's nursing a joey in her pouch; if something happens to the joey, the blastocyst seems to serve as a ready backup unit.

Small animals typically have very short gestation periods. It appears that delayed implantation may be the only way they can arrange to give birth in the optimal season, especially if that season occurs during or at the end of an extended period of environmental stress, such as winter. One species of bat appears to have developed a slightly different form of delay, in that the growth of the egg does not completely stop; it just goes very slowly, gradually accelerating late in the fetus's term.

Even having said all this, I've only given you a sort of *Reader's Digest* condensed essay summary here. The scientists I've been reading are deep into discussions of the biochemistry of all this, the subtle effects of changing photoperiods, and lots of other rewarding matters. The best questions always lead to more questions. There are bats who have taken a whole different approach: they mate in fall and winter, but they delay fertilization rather than implantation. The females store live sperm in their uteri for up to ten weeks before ovulating, so that the sperm have something to fertilize. Imagine the convenience. Romantic hedonists have it that variety is the spice of life; whether or not that is true, variety is surely the essence of reproductive biology.

Jeremy Schmidt, a travel-writer friend of mine, recently wrote that "the earth works wonders and holds them secret." He might have added that it's all the same to the earth whether or not we ever figure them out, or even if we notice. There are always new secrets, but the harder we look, and the more questions we answer, the more obscure and hazy the new secrets become.

Perhaps that's another reason I spend so much time seeking out the old questions. The biologists now studying delayed implantation are asking questions so technical that I can barely follow them.

Perhaps that's also why for so long we've heard so little about delayed implantation in popular magazines and books; questions of physiology and biochemistry still don't have the public appeal that more visible animal traits do. I'd hate to think, though, that one of the nineteenth century's most intriguing wildlife questions— where are all the pregnant bears?—should reach a dead end of public interest just because the answer isn't simple enough, or easily enough illustrated with color photographs in a nature magazine, to appeal to us today.

I'd better let it go at that, before this essay degenerates into a polemic on the national crisis of scientific illiteracy that has never before been so painfully exposed as it was in 2020. What the discovery of delayed implantation teaches us, and what Jeremy was politely saying, is that the earth works wonders and holds them secret only until we have enough impatience with our own ignorance to try to figure them out.

9

Ferocious Beasts

Near the conclusion of the wonderful adventure movie *Romancing the Stone*, the Arch Bad Guy stood on the shore of a tropical harbor, triumphantly clutching the priceless gem that had absorbed the attention of the entire cast for nearly two hours. Just then, in mid-gloat, he was attacked by a huge alligator, which poked its head out of the water and neatly chomped off and swallowed the hand holding the gem. In that moment a significant amount of cinematic justice was done, and a few moments later this same hard-luck villain, now also bleeding from a gruesome eyeball wound and (for good measure) generally aflame, fell into a deep pit containing some other alligators, where he was justly consumed, tastefully off-camera. Thus with the timely support of a few alligators the Good Guys, and especially Kathleen Turner, won the day.

But let's go back to that first alligator. While alligators are known to remove limbs from their prey, it doesn't happen much like it did in the movie. Alligators have pointy, fanglike teeth along the sides of their jaws. These teeth are great for clamping onto things but they aren't all that hot at slicing something off of something else. If the alligator wanted to remove the hand or the arm, it would have done so by gripping it with those big teeth, dragging the Arch Bad Guy into the water, and then twisting around until the combination of torque, tearing, and pulling brought the limb free.

I don't introduce this bit of cinematic excess for any weird joy of discussing such bloody messes. I find it revealing in more important ways, because it says a lot about our willingness to ascribe remarkable powers to animals that we routinely think of as ferocious.

Ferocity in nature is a cherished social concept. Wildernesses howl, wolves are ravenous, sharks are just downright horrible. Anything—oar, hand, foot, pet, child, and other personal bits— left exposed over the edge of anything else—boat, bridge, dock, shoreline—is liable to disappear into a ferocious mouth. As small children (well, some of us, anyway), we are careful not to let a foot or hand dangle over the edge of the bed, for fear of the ferocious menagerie of imaginary carnivores (mine were, for some inexplicable reason, giant weasels) that roamed the floor after the lights went out. Vicious bears, vindictive rattlesnakes, snarling lions, and simply vile crocodilians stalked the pages of some of our favorite storybooks, and still survive in robust breeding populations in many modern outdoor magazines, filling readers with ecstatic loathings. This may be our fullest love-hate relationship with nature.

At first glance, a stranger to all this thrilling revulsion might look at the bear and wonder where it fits. While sharks, alligators, snakes, tigers, and even wolves all have a sleek, lithe look about them, bears are, well, round. And furry. With cute little ears. And though modern toymakers have given us—among many other startling things—fuzzy, cuddly gators, sharks, and even velociraptors(!), those creatures' real counterparts out in the world's ancient and modern forests and oceans rarely inspire anyone to say, "Don't you just wanna hug him?" Many of us do say, or at least feel, that way when we see bears, and not just cubs. A male grizzly bear lumbering along minding his own business and showing no indication whatsoever of how quickly, given the mood, he could abruptly chase and overtake some four- or two-legged animal and crush its skull, can look about as threatening and almost as inviting as your favorite old sofa.

But that's how it is with bears; here we are, coming at their complications from yet another direction. In *The Sacred Paw: The Bear in Nature, Myth, and Literature* (1985), Paul Shepard and Barry Sanders put it like this:

Vol. 2.] "GO AHEAD!!" [No. 3.

THE CROCKETT ALMANAC 1841.

Tussel with a Bear. See page 9.

Containing Adventures, Exploits, Sprees & Scrapes in the West, & Life and Manners in the Backwoods.

Nashville, Tennessee. Published by Ben Harding.

23. For much of our history of dealing with bears we have characterized them invariably as reflexively violent. Eastern black bears, like the ones David Crockett rassled in legend, were routinely portrayed with a combination of wolfish and grizzlyish features—often with a bit of alligator tossed in. Photo by author.

Versatile in meaning as he is, in his natural state, the bear is many things to men: the stuffed Teddy and Pooh of childhood fantasy, the shambling, morose clown of the circus, the huckster and caricature of cartoons, the terrifying monster of the forest and arctic ice, the prince of game animals, the grandmother in mythic kinship to humans, a constellation marking the passage of the night, the season and the cycle of life, a symbol of the Church, and a powerful spirit who mediates between man and a forest god.

Right. Traditional views of most of nature's "monsters" haven't allowed for such diversity of personality, such a buffet of symbolism wrapped up in one mammalian package (on its best days the wolf may come close, depending in good part on who is talking about it). And all that being said, where does ferocity fit in?

It should be clear from the previous chapters that I don't for a minute question the reality of what wild animals do to each other, much less what they occasionally to do people. Almost anything alive in the woods today might be eaten by something else tomorrow (or tonight, darkness seeming to be when ferocity is most often rampant). What I question, in fact what I have come to reject, is this whole business of describing some species as ferocious in the first place.

Webster tells me that ferocious means "having or exhibiting ferocity, cruelty, savagery, etc.; violently cruel, as ferocious actions or looks." That seems straightforward enough. It describes some types of human behavior—war, for instance, or the most intense forms of bullying—quite well. But does it really serve as an accurate description of other animals?

Though in recent decades we've made a lot of progress away from our older ways of seeing these creatures, there are a few North American mammals that we traditionally and routinely consider ferocious: bears, cougars, wolves, wolverines, and the like, including some surprisingly small ones. I suppose anybody who has attempted to cross a pasture inhabited by a big bull, tried to ride an especially hostile horse, or met up with a large and violently territorial watchdog, would be inclined to add them to this list, but for the most part the ferocious beasts we picture in our minds are wild carnivores, or at least omnivores. So if by ferocious we mean "can be expected to try to kill or even eat other animals," then these animals would qualify. But if by "ferocious" we mean "characterized by an inherent cruelty and malice," or "taking joy in causing pain to others," then we're on thin behavioral ice.

I have a strong hunch that some, and maybe all, predators must feel some kind of elemental satisfaction or even exhilaration in capturing their prey. It is to their great evolutionary advantage that they find the experience of predation to be, in some deep and compelling sense, rewarding. Hunger or the need to feed young may be itself incentive enough to get the bear out there looking for elk calves, but the additional incentive of an exciting hunt and kill may provide much additional reward.

But I doubt that the thrill of the chase has anything to do with cruelty for its own sake. These animals have spent millions of years becoming as efficient as possible at killing, and killing is a biological function, whatever else it may be. A bear may use similar shearing-and-tearing motions with its teeth whether it is grazing a meadow or separating meat from an elk carcass. Rarely, if ever, is there any evolutionary gain for the predator in causing a prey animal physical pain beyond that necessary to acquire and consume it. A bear is not encumbered by human concepts of good sportsmanship, but it has every reason to make an efficient kill.

And yet, in fairness to our human sensitivities, it's not that simple, is it? It is in fact complicated, for us as observers, at least, by the messier realities of predation.

For one thing, to serve its purposes, all the predator must do is immobilize its prey; once that is accomplished, it seems generally irrelevant to the predator whether or not the prey is actually dead. As long as the captured and still-living prey doesn't struggle enough to interfere with the predator's feeding on it, the predator doesn't mind. I think I speak for most of us when I say that sounds like a pretty horrible way to go; make that burger well done, please.

For another, some predators—perhaps most famously, cats— "play" with their prey once they've captured it; at first glance this

24. Another grizzlified black bear, this one in Indiana, from Charles Major's 1901 *The Bears of Blue River*.

looks to us a lot like torture. Some of those same predators may teach their young to kill prey by letting them similarly play with a captured prey, which according to our values would be torture for educational reasons; is that less, uh, wrong?

Then there's that ever-popular complaint among people who strongly disapprove of predators, that some of them indulge in "surplus killing," or even "joy killing," that is, killing a lot more than they would seem to have any use for. We must ask, what's the point then? What good does that frenzy do you?

All these activities, however well they may work for the predator, are hard for us to watch without an emotional reaction, nor should we necessarily deny ourselves such a reaction. But modern behavioral studies have offered a number of possible explanations that go a long way to explaining these seemingly "cruel" or "wasteful" predation behaviors, not in terms that satisfy our human moral systems but in terms that work not just for the predator but for the predator's world.

We are learning to ask ourselves new and often hard questions of the "What's really going on here?" variety. What possible practical advantage is it for the bear to care to finish off a disabled, dying, and immobile elk before starting to consume it? It's a bear. It's hungry, and it has a straightforward view of what to do about it.

And the house cat that repeatedly engages in "catch and release" with a mouse? It's a cat. It doesn't put a high premium on the cuteness of mice. Maybe it's just a cat that rarely gets an opportunity to activate its profound and deeply instinctive urge to hunt and is therefore simply unable to resist this rare chance to practice its predatory trade (anglers among us, including me, may cringe if we compare this behavior to catch-and-release fishing, but there it is.)

Or consider so-called surplus killing from a longer view. Two hundred years ago, many human hunters in America routinely killed a great many deer or elk or ducks or any other species of wildlife in a day. This sort of slaughter was often a cause for celebration in the neighborhood. Today, for a variety of good, practical reasons, we are shocked by the very idea of such a bloodbath, and sensible hunter-conservationists rightly deplore any waste of a valuable game animal.

But "waste" itself is a tricky term, especially when the killed prey may be fed on for days or weeks by the predator, and are also available to a host of secondary consumers, from scavenging vultures to dozens if not hundreds of species of insects and microorganisms (and again for the anglers—one of the twentieth century's foremost angler-conservationists, Lee Wulff, asserted that a game fish is too valuable to be caught only once, which was to say that killing that fish the first time it's caught was a waste of a valuable recreational resource).

For example, why should we expect the grizzly bear who was lounging on the bison carcass back in chapter 4 to finish its meal in one sitting, when it's a sure thing that in a few days, weeks, or months, the whole carcass will be reduced to a few bleaching bones, possibly with a thick feltlike mat of bison hair pressed into the ground around it? The questions and answers we are now working through about these behaviors may never satisfy our own ideas of right and wrong, but we shouldn't expect them to.

There's another element to this matter, and that's empathy. Ferocity is a characteristic we mostly tend to ascribe to those animals that are hunting either us or species we care about. Our conception of ferocity has as much to do with who is being eaten as with who is doing the eating. We may be tearfully disturbed watching a coyote kill a deer, but we invariably enjoy watching a barn swallow wheeling about over a pond consuming countless beaksful of newly hatched mayflies. The swallow, a lovely little animal traditionally associated with tender affections, has just killed hundreds of its fellow creatures—and few animals have a more exquisite grace and beauty than adult mayflies—but they are creatures we never see closely enough to care much about. Is the swallow's behavior any less aggressive, violent, or destructive of individual lives than the coyote's? No, most of us just don't have any sympathy for the mayflies, who are "just bugs" anyway. We would have a whole different take on the lovely swallows if they had twelve-foot wingspans and were hauling off our poodles and children.

Over the course of the past few centuries, we've tried on a remarkable assortment of attitudes about animal personalities. At some stages of our thinking, a purely mechanistic outlook has prevailed, wherein all animals were seen as fundamentally thoughtless automatons that reacted mindlessly to their surroundings. At other stages, we've binged on anthropomorphism, equating animal actions more or less precisely with corresponding human actions. Most of the time, no matter what view the majority of us adopted, we were still weighing down the animals with our own moral freight.

Historian Keith Thomas aptly summarized one stage in this evolving idea of animals as it stood in sixteenth-century England:

Men attributed to animals the natural impulses they most feared in themselves—ferocity, gluttony, sexuality—even though it was men, not beasts, who made war on their own species, ate more than was good for them and were sexually active all the year round. It was a comment on *human* nature that the concept of "animality" was devised. As S. T. Coleridge would observe, to call human vices "bestial" was to libel the animals.

I don't mean to suggest that we haven't made a lot of progress since the 1500s. Gradually we have reached a more realistic balance in how we view animals. But most of us still carry a pretty heavy load of value judgments, and there is probably little harm in that. I am personally certain, for example, that the obnoxious dog that lives across the alley is not simply a poorly trained animal cursed with stupid owners; he is a jerk.

The popular view of predators as mean-spirited villains, pervasive as it still is in many parts of human culture, is unfortunate. I, for one, would have been happier if, at the end of *Romancing the Stone*, the alligator had behaved more realistically and just dragged the Bad Guy under, providing an opportunity for one of the most dramatic of cinematic deaths: the churning tropical pool that becomes ominously still. It certainly would have been a fitting end for the ferocious villain.

10

Bear Attacks

An Appreciation

L ater on I will turn to the question of favorite bear books, which seems to me, now that I think about it, a much safer and more answerable question than trying to identify, say, the "best" bear books. As to the latter, who says? We all have favorites, and for each of us those favorites may even amount to our idea of the best. But how could there be a best bear book for all of us? The many existing bear books come at the idea and reality of bears from so many perspectives, and with such a diversity of opinion and intention, that there seems no point in even trying to set up such a standard. How could one book be measurably better, and by what possible measure, than all the others?

A perhaps fairer question, on the other hand, may be this: is there a most *important* bear book? Again, it's easy to bog down in the bear literature's variety and end up with a hopeless quandary: "most important" to whom?

But there is one book that has proven to be important in so many vital ways—to the bears, to their admirers, their researchers, and their managers—that it may well deserve such a sweeping characterization. It is our society's best shot at coming up with a book that, even if we may quibble over its preeminence among all others, we cannot doubt its extraordinary and unparalleled usefulness. It sometimes seems to me to be the book that generations of bear-book authors have been working toward, and I turn to it now because it has so recently, just in 2018, been republished.

The appearance of a new edition of Dr. Stephen Herrero's *Bear*

25. The author (*right*) with this book's dedicatees, Linda Wiggins and Steve Herrero, watching for wildlife in Yellowstone's Slough Creek Valley. Photo courtesy of the author.

Attacks: Their Causes and Avoidance is a cause for great celebration among everyone who cares about bears and the wild country they inhabit and symbolize. In half a century of exploring the scientific and popular literature of bears, I have found no other publication that has done as much to illuminate the world of the wild bear, or to inspire in readers the necessary fortitude and commitment needed to respect, preserve, and get along with these precious animals. Much more than a guide to living safely in bear country, it is an incomparable introduction to the complete bear: how they live, why they behave the way they do, and why they are so important to us.

I first became aware of Steve Herrero's work more than forty years ago while working on the first edition of *The Bears of Yellowstone*. Even among the outstanding, if still small, group of researchers then pioneering bear science, Steve's writings on bears revealed a special depth of understanding—not only of the ecology and behavior of bears but also of their powerful meaning to human society. In fact, my book featured as an opening epigram the following statement from one of Steve's early scientific papers, "We should preserve grizzly bear populations, not because their ecological function is critical, but because of what they can do for human imagination, thought, and experience."

Then came Steve's book, *Bear Attacks: Their Causes and Avoidance*, first published in 1985. I can best illustrate its impact on modern thinking about bears with the following story. In 1992, it was my honor to serve as coeditor, with U.S. Forest Service biologist James Claar, of the proceedings of the ninth international conference on bear research and management, held that year in Missoula, Montana. The lead paper in this generous scientific compendium was written by National Park Service biologist Clifford Martinka and featured the results of a survey he conducted among many professionals in the world of bear research and management, asking them to list the five outstanding bear-related publications of the previous twenty-five years. Cliff then compiled the "votes" and presented the eleven top-ranked publications in his paper.

Cliff's list reads like a who's who in bear research at the time: Jonkel, Rogers, Craighead, another equally important Craighead, Stirling, Pearson, and others. But by far the most frequently named publication was *Bear Attacks: Their Causes and Avoidance*, by Stephen Herrero, which these leading bear professionals listed 50 percent more often than the second-place publication.

It's hard to overstate what a remarkable achievement this was. Though only in print a few years, and though written for a popular audience, *Bear Attacks* had already achieved a uniquely authoritative status among the foremost bear researchers and managers. Steve's work was further recognized in his election to the presidency of the International Association for Bear Research and Management (1985–87) and his appointment as chair of the International Union for the Conservation of Nature's Bear Specialist Group (1986–90).

There's a fun irony about Steve's eminence as a bear authority that I should also share. In chapter 3 I discuss Benjamin Kilham's splendid book *Out on a Limb: What Black Bears Taught Me about Intelligence and Intuition*, first published in 2013. Back when I was shopping for that book, I dutifully read through the numerous promotional quotes written by various notables on behalf of the book, and it is indeed quite a list. I suspect, however, that quite a few other devoted bear enthusiasts probably had a reaction something like mine. The blurbs come from some very famous people, and I read through the endorsements thinking, "Elizabeth Thomas, that's a swell quote to have; and, oh, here's George Schaller, that's an endorsement any nature writer would love to have," and so on. At the very end of the group of quotes, buried at the bottom of the second page, was this one: "Kilham's latest is the most thought-provoking book that I've read about bears. It not only made me think differently about black bears, it also enriched how I feel about them." This brief assertion—the shortest of all the blurbs—was from Steve Herrero, and as soon as I read it I thought, "Oh, well, then—Steve likes it; I really have to read it."

The irony there is of course that the publisher preceded what is by far the most meaningful testimonial—at least for serious followers of bear science and literature—with a bunch of apparently more famous names. I don't doubt that this approach may have been good marketing, especially among the general public. But it ended up hiding the most authoritative and trustworthy quote of all.

Steve and I have often crossed paths since *Bear Attacks* first came out. He generously agreed to participate in my 1990 and 1991 grizzly bear ecology and management courses at the Yellowstone Institute, where his profound understanding of bear-human relationships was no doubt as fascinating to my students as it was to me. Whether out on some hillside with spotting scopes, or in one-on-one conversations at home, or in front of any audience small or large, Steve is not only an insightful authority on bears; he is a wise and sympathetic teacher and an eloquent advocate for protecting the wonders of the natural world.

And as this new edition shows, the unique and commanding stature of his book continues to grow. Dog-eared copies of *Bear Attacks*, many smudged and rumpled from riding in backpacks and being studied by the light of countless campfires, inhabit the shelves of tens of thousands of grateful bear-country travelers. Today *Bear Attacks* remains a uniquely helpful welcome to the world of bears, and I envy you your first reading of it. Take its wisdom to heart and the magic of bear country will always be yours.

The Question Answered

As I've already said, grizzly bear country invites you to participate in a rich and thriving folklore, a near mythology of nature that humans have constructed around the bear. Every sign of a bear, no matter how peripheral or central to the bear's life, provides you a link into that world, whether it scares the devil out of you, stirs your soul, or just gives you a laugh.

One day at the Goat Haunt trailhead in Glacier National Park I overheard some hikers excitedly reporting to a ranger about a pile of bear scat they'd found a few miles back up the trail. The ranger calmly answered their questions, and agreed with their wide-eyed assertions that, yes, sometimes the piles are "REALLY BIG!" But he finally had to explain that there's only so much you can tell about a bear from just seeing a pile of its poop.

They were a little let down by the failure of their description of this particular poop pile to provide a complete biography of the bear that produced it, but after a moment's thought, one of them said, "It does, however, answer the age-old question."

On Skipping The Revenant

When we go to a movie, many of us find it difficult not to play critic. Some of us, with the inveterate amateur's blithe overconfidence, go in for analysis of the refined aesthetic and technical elements of the cinematic arts. Lighting, sound, camera perspectives, continuity, script quality, fidelity to whatever unfortunate book the movie is based on, and a host of other mysterious parts of acting and filmmaking all undergo intense scrutiny.

But I suppose for most of us—and now I'm talking about me—criticism is limited to simpler matters, like how could they get this or that really obvious thing so wrong? Though we know that expending any energy whatsoever on second-guessing and gotcha-ing the people who make movies serves no noticeable greater good, doing so may be one of society's foremost smugness generators. Next to criticizing politicians, where else can we get so much happy reinforcement of our belief that we're smarter than someone else—especially rich and internationally adored someones like movie stars and directors? I mean to say, politicians are such easy targets after all, and sometimes we yearn for more challenging game.

But as we embrace this sweet and delusional opportunity for self-approval, our long-suffering spouses and friends must often wonder: Who cares? More to the point, what good does it do to indignantly announce, as you're watching the movie, that the actor has just described his Glock 19 semiautomatic pistol as a "revolver?" How does it benefit humanity—or, more specifically, the people around you in the theater or next to you in your living room—to express spirited exasperation that in some rousing London car chase the driver just turned a corner out of Trafalgar Square to immediately bounce down the Spanish Steps before getting caught in the perpetual bumper-to-bumper traffic snarl around the Arc de Triomphe before making a hard right and winding down Lombard Street? It's just a movie for Pete's sake, and if it has a car chase in it in the first place it's almost certainly just a stupendously expensive live-action comic book featuring sticky floors and twelve-dollar candy bars. Why should we take it any more seriously than its makers did?

And yet like so many other quixotic world-improvers, I still have a hard time not getting exercised by the fast-and-loose ways of movies. Sometimes I remind myself of that dumpy bald professorial fellow in a long-ago *New Yorker* cartoon who, in a theater full of children watching spaceships in spectacular battle, suddenly jumps up shouting, "Stop the movie! Stop the movie! Explosions don't go boom in a vacuum!"

Other times I heave myself up onto the High Road of Scholarly Rectitude, from which lofty eminence I scoff (from lofty eminences one must scoff rather than merely laugh) at a cheesy cinematic treatment of some beloved work of literature (did a book as beautifully written and richly peopled as *The Hobbit* really need a slinky elf-chick-warrior?).

Having said all that—and having *not* said a great deal more that clamors to escape from my brain's movie-grumping files—I don't hesitate to admit that I love movies. I seem to be as happy watching the glitchy, anachronism-ridden ones as I am with the masterpieces of brilliant filmmaking, and I don't hesitate to admit that I'm not always sure I can tell one from the other.

Of course this rumination can lead nowhere else (you may be wondering by now) but to bears. For many years there, when I was reading intensively about everything to do with bears, I felt it was also my duty to watch every available movie about bears—not only all the earnest television documentaries but also bigger-budget, real-theater movies. And, looking back now, I suppose that this experience was a part of my early education in how movies may or may not offer viewers anything trustworthy or even accurate about their subject. On the other hand, bear movies certainly gave us the full flavor of all the things that bears can mean to us. From the Craighead brothers' vivid and inspiring National Geographic documentaries about their pioneering Yellowstone grizzly bear research to the silliest guy-in-a-ratty-bear-suit monster movies, I could, as the song said, "see it all there."

And most of the time as I watched, I remembered that whatever the movie's director and stars were up to, bears are bears, by definition enchanting to watch. In that frame of mind, just the chance to get such extended looks at movie bears doing whatever movie bears might be trained to do was novel enough to overshadow most concerns I might have had about accuracy. After all, a bear moving around doing bearish things on a movie set is still a bear moving around doing bearish things. Who can tire of watching bear cubs being bear cubs, whether it's on a movie set or out in the woods?

Eventually, after most of my bear books were published and my writing about bears tapered off, I felt less and less obligated to see each new film, though in the past few years I have made an exception for giant pandas. I can't resist any new online film clip of baby pandas. I eagerly and repeatedly watch each new video from wherever it is in China where they now have dozens of captive young pandas. How could I not? How could anyone not? Besides the exhilaration of seeing such a luxurious abundance of the babies of a species so long threatened with extinction, baby pandas are somewhere well off the top of all known adorability scales. The only thing that could make it better is if I could be assured that the *wild* panda populations were likewise booming and having just as much fun. Apparently not, but I can only hope.

So lately, people I know have been insisting that I go see the 2015 movie *The Revenant*, the most recent retelling of the famous story of bear-mauling victim Hugh Glass—It's great, they exclaim, it's so realistic and so exciting, it's the real thing, it makes history come alive, and all that sort of enthusiastic talk. You have to go see it, Paul!

As most western history enthusiasts know, Glass, a mountain man in the 1820s American West, was horribly and comprehensively mauled by a grizzly bear. Eventually left for dead (or, in the minds of his pragmatic and harried companions, dead enough as made no difference), Glass somehow survived and his agonizing solo crawl/walk a couple hundred miles to the nearest settlement became one of the most famous episodes in the long history of North American human–grizzly bear encounters. It is an astonishing story, and for a great many people Glass has become a figure of Homeric proportions, an archetypical American hero. As historian John Myers summed him up in *The Saga of Hugh Glass*, "Deep in the Medicine Bag of every nation is the tale of a warrior pitted against a beast of dread proportions. In the lore of America, this alpha of epics takes the form of a struggle between a mountain man called Hugh Glass and an outsize grizzly." Certainly the people who insisted that I must see the movie didn't know any of this, but considering my well-known interest in bears, I can see why people might think I should go see such a movie.

I didn't need to give these suggestions much thought, at least not at first. I just said no thanks, explaining that I knew the Hugh Glass story pretty well from all the retellings—fictional, poetic, and assorted quasi-nonfiction—it has undergone during the past two centuries or so. Besides, I'd read about the movie and understood that besides the graphic portrayal of the awful injuries sustained by Glass (to say nothing of the death of the bear), it also featured another brutal scene in which a swinish mountain man rapes a Native American woman. So, no thanks.

To my surprise and bewilderment, this wasn't a good enough answer. I must go see it! Don't be a wimp! Man up!

I didn't respond to such commands. I let the conversations drop and hoped the whole thing would go away. But it didn't, and I haven't yet been able to get it out of my mind. Given some time to think it over, here is how I see my situation.

First, I don't think this is merely about my angst over Hollywood's tradition of willfully misrepresenting everything to do with ecological realities. So maybe, instead, it's just me taking offense at the forceful implication that this movie is somehow going to broaden my bear horizons, or smarten me up, or in some other unexpected way reward my time and expense for watching it; or, worse, the even less savory implication that I'm chickening out by not going to see the real thing so vividly portrayed. Did they just hurt my feelings?

Could be, I guess. Doubt it, though.

From that highly ambivalent stance, I launch this little rumination. One thing I've learned for sure about writing is that getting something down on paper almost always clarifies or even advances my thinking about it. Sometimes, even if all else fails, it enables me to let it go. So here goes. Why am I so confident about not needing to see this movie?

First, I'll go after the *human* brutality. Over the years I've known a few rape victims, and I long ago formulated a firm perspective on anyone who would force himself sexually on another person. That perspective is based on pained and tearful realities I have heard from rape victims and isn't likely ever to require reinforcement from Hollywood.

Besides, you'll never convince me that the rape scene in that movie was there for the sake of historical authenticity. It was placed there to sell movie tickets to people who in some way or another need to see such a scene. I could go on and on about this, but a bear book isn't quite the place for it, so I'll move on to poor old Hugh Glass and his famously bad day.

In my reading I've come across Glass's story many times. He never wrote about it himself, or if he did, his version has not surfaced. But stories by others started to appear in the 1820s and obviously still have great currency today. From a handful of actual bits of possibly firsthand information left by a few mountain men and the people they told about it, generation after generation of writers has retold, enlarged upon, and otherwise fancied up the story until it, like so many historical episodes, has taken on a mythic life of its own.

26. Sculptor John Lopez's historic monument *Hugh Glass and Grizzly* is a spectacular recent interpretation of what is possibly the most famous of all historic encounters between grizzly bear and man. The monument is on permanent display at the Grand River Museum in Lemmon, South Dakota, not far from the site of the legendary episode that proved fatal for the bear and nearly so for Glass. Courtesy of John Lopez.

In addition to these short renderings of the tale almost beyond counting, there have been several books, including the novel on which the new movie is based. The authors of these books sometimes struggled to set aside the historical chaff and get back to what might surely be known about what happened that day, doing just what Myers's book was all about (we can look back now and see that his review of the Glass literature holds up much better than does his grasp of bear natural history). Besides all these publications, *The Revenant* is by no means the first film take on the Glass story, and the more thoughtful reviews of the movie do point out its many fictional flourishes, and its embroideries of the little that is known about the historical events involved (because I didn't feel any need to read the novel upon which it is based, either, I have no idea how well it handles the story).

If I was still writing the sort of bear books I used to, I probably would have felt compelled to sit through the movie, just for a professional look at the latest twists and turns this endlessly flexible narrative has taken, or for what the movie might inadvertently tell me about how grizzly bears are perceived in today's filmmaking circles, or how they are "enjoyed" by the public. But no, I don't have any need to absorb the latest product from the Hugh Glass Saga Industry. I know enough about how this process works to suit me.

For upward of half a century now, bears—not only the real ones that lived in the wild country all around me but the countless *ideas* of bears that millennia of human societies around the world have imagined and celebrated—have been one of the most lively and deeply rewarding natural history focuses of my life. I've never claimed to be an expert on bear biology or behavior, but I've spent a great deal of time with such people and we've talked a lot about the very complicated business of violence between bears and humans.

More important, living and working where I have all that time, I've read the official reports and personal narratives of rangers and scientists involved in cleaning up the sites of bear maulings, and I've seen more official photographs of the human remains of bear attacks than I care to remember. I've known several mauling victims, seen their scars and heard their stories. In one memorable instance, I was walked around the site of a then very recent fatal bear attack by a savvy veteran bear researcher who read for me the vivid signs of what happened to that particular person in the final terrifying moments of his life.

Perhaps more important than all that, I've been fortunate enough not only to see bears hunt and kill other nonhuman animals, but also to see the highly informative leftovers of such predations.

Perhaps most important of all, I've put in my own time with the bears, including hundreds of hours watching for them and observing them, often in places where the bear might just as likely appear right behind me as show up in the pleasantly comfortable distance in front of me. I've hiked, ridden, or otherwise traveled many, many very exciting miles in various parts of North America from the Far North to the former grizzly bear country of northern Mexico. And though I'm quite sure that my trail mileage totals are sadly tiny by the standards of professional researchers or hardcore bear-country hikers, those miles were profoundly important to me. I was out there where, besides all the unforgettable glory and wonder that always comes with time in wild country, I had abundant opportunity to consider just what would happen if, at any given moment on any given trail, I ran into a bear. Among the many other things that I recall from all those happy trail days is the frequent and always dismaying realization that even in the dense, tall forests of the American West it is shocking how rarely there is a tree nearby whose architecture looks cooperative enough that I might be able to climb it if I suddenly had to escape a hypothetical bear who was suddenly all too real, and thundering my way. All I could do was hope that the inspiration—read "terror"—of the moment would assist me in climbing even an inhospitable tree.

These considerations were about as vivid and nonabstract as could be, and I have always been unspeakably grateful to the bears I did encounter for their patience and forbearance (so to speak) as I humbly extracted myself from their presence. And I was just as grateful to the much larger number of bears that I didn't even notice but who, I am sure, discreetly watched me go by.

And another thing. While I'm clearing the bear air here, I'm fed up to the back teeth with the obligatory references so many writers fall back on, to the "razor sharp" teeth and claws of the big predators. Wolves, lions, and God knows what all else are portrayed as going through their days with Schick-ish blades sticking out of their paws and jaws. In the present instance I'm thinking of someone-or-other's very recently published description of the "razor-like talons" of the bear that did such an effective number on Glass. Setting aside the problem that "talon" is a term almost exclusively applied to the feet of birds (and dragons, I guess), this makes no sense.

There are good evolutionary reasons why these animals' teeth and claws are not, in fact, razor sharp. For one thing, they would be a lot less durable. Considering what all a hardworking predator must do with its teeth and claws, a razor edge wouldn't last long. Bears do lots of digging, tearing apart of logs, and other serious contractor-grade work that would blunt and quickly snap a fine-edged claw. It's not easy chewing through a thick bison hide, or crunching the heavy long bones of an elk to get at the goodies inside. Bears need robust, durable equipment for their work and for their dining. I defy anyone who thinks these excellent natural

27. *Unwelcome Encounter*, from John C. Van Tramp, *Prairie and Rocky Mountain Adventures*. Any nineteenth-century book of adventures in the wilds of the American West almost had to contain one or more stories about encounters with bears—whether humorous, desperate, heroic, or tragic. The following sampling of illustrations from these tales reveals their variety.

28. Uncaptioned image of a Native American man fighting grizzly bears, from Washington Irving, *The Adventures of Captain Bonneville*.

29. *Attack of a Grizzly Bear*, from T. D. Bonner, *The Life and Adventures of James P. Beckwourth.*

30. Uncaptioned ornamental scene from Jules Verne's novel *The Fur Country.*

31. Uncaptioned but obviously complicated bear adventure from Mayne Reid, *The Boy Hunters*.

32. and **33.** Humorous pair of bear-hunting scenes entitled *Jack Loaded for Bear* and *Bear Loaded for Jack*, from George Oliver Shields, *Hunting in the Great West*.

weapons and tools are "razor sharp" to take a closer look at them and then imagine shaving any part of his or her body with one.

Moviegoing, like moviemaking, is an imperfect art. I suspect that even if I didn't have this whole self-serving armory of personal acquaintance with the bear and its world to back me up, I'd still not want to see *The Revenant* just because it doesn't sound like fun. At my dismayingly advanced age, fun—at least as I define it—is a higher priority for me than it's ever been before. So for my moviegoing pleasure I'll stick with spaceships blowing up with lots of big booms—and I'll happily live with the ironies of that choice.

All this fuming and harumphing on my part is probably some indication that I take even ignorant assessments of my interest in bears much more seriously than I should (and here I am, taking it out on you). I even suspect that in the above rant I have succumbed to some gotcha-ish smugness of my own in my indignant if not self-righteous exposure of pop culture's occasional worst moments in their generally enjoyable celebrations of bears.

So what have I learned? Where do I go with this little exercise in sorting out my restlessness about what is, really, just another movie? Well, the overwhelming temptation at this point is the rhetorical one, in which I (1) launch my wrap-up with the nearly obligatory panoramic exhalations about the bear's rich symbolic role in our society and the need to be flexible in appreciating our ever-evolving perspective on these magically engaging animals; or (2) deplore our deep urges to swing into full-tilt, faux-mountain-man, armchair-machismo when we discuss them big ol' grizzlies; or (3) emphasize our need to curtail our least savory emotional appetites when we are subjected to yet another sensational portrayal of bears; or (4) just point out yet again and to absolutely no one's interest, much less surprise, that Hollywood can turn any good story into crap; even though, not having seen *The Revenant*, I don't know to what extent that's true.

But this just doesn't feel like an occasion to get all literary. I like to think I've said some fairly useful and possibly even entertaining things here, so I'll just thank you for letting me get it out of my system and let it go at that.

THREE

Alaska

13

Denali Days

By 1998 I had been what I liked to think of as a serious wildlife watcher for more than twenty-five years. Under the tutelage of a few experts, I became consciously part of a small but passionate school of park visitor–wildlife watchers that was emerging in Yellowstone and, I imagine, in many other parks and wild places. As I've already said, in the years since the 1960s, as bears and other animals were divorced from human food sources—random ice chests, garbage cans and dumps, gherkin-lobbing motorists, hiker's backpacks, sandwich-laden picnic tables—and the animals were compelled to redistribute themselves where wild foods were most available, wildlife watching in the parks became a more challenging and *much* more rewarding exercise. And in Yellowstone, the arrival of wolves, reintroduced amid roaring (or, better, howling) public controversy and growing excitement in 1995, greatly increased public enthusiasm for watching wild nature.

The techniques for watching weren't really new, of course. We, the most recent generation of wildlife watchers, were just learning what a few professional naturalists, bird watchers, and sportsmen knew all along, that wildlife watching can be more than driving the road in the hopes of happening upon an animal in view. It is a matter of understanding the animal's world, of hard work getting to the right places at the right times, and of patience. The understanding and the hard work are fairly straightforward and easy enough to come by; the patience is not.

The finer points of this new approach to wildlife appreciation took a while to catch on and will probably never appeal to most visitors, who have neither the time nor the inclination to settle in among the ticks and mosquitoes for a few hours, just looking at a big landscape until some animal or other wanders into view. But for the dedicated enthusiast, whether gifted professional or determined amateur, putting in hundreds or even thousands of hours with binoculars and spotting scopes and applying what science and personal experience have taught us about how bears behave and what bears eat, to figure out where the bears will be and when they will be there has been enormously fulfilling.

I had and occasionally still have my own favorite places for doing this, hills from which I can look out across thousands of acres of wildland. With low-power optics for scanning and high-power optics for closer observation once I've found something, I've learned to identify and enjoy wild mammals as far as four miles off. At four miles, if you have enough practice, it is often possible to distinguish a black bear from a grizzly and tell a great deal about what it is doing. With my modest and fairly cheap scope, I've located and identified bears at up to six miles away, but even in the dry West there is too much heat distortion in such a great stretch of air for any serious observation.

So though I never claimed to be a master at this, I did put in enough hours to become competent, and a little proud of my skills. There are times when nature is so generous you can't help getting an inflated view of your woodcraft. I first learned this as a fisherman, when a day with lots of catching was most likely to be followed by several days with lots of casting. Likewise, there were days when the bears seemed to line up to show off for me. Even as I enjoyed such a treat, I knew the odds were good that I might sit and wait for several days before nature bothered to show me even a single bored coyote recreationally scratching itself.

Then in 1998 came my first trip to Alaska, and it was in this same enthusiastic and somewhat overwrought mood that I approached wildlife watching there, in a place that meant a lot to me even before I got there.

During all those years in and out of Yellowstone, Glacier, and

34. Grizzly country, Denali National Park, Alaska. Photo by author.

many other wild places all over the Lower 48, I often thought about Alaska. Sometimes I thought of working in some park there, sometimes I just imagined taking a few months and going up there on the cheap, camping, hiking, fishing, and otherwise exploring all those magnificent places I'd heard and read so much about.

Like so many good things in my life, going to Alaska happened because of my wife, Marsha. A career National Park Service professional, she began her park work in Denali in 1981. After a season working in the restaurant for the concessioner at park headquarters—a job she quit because she didn't like walking home through grizzly country every day "smelling like a French fry"—she landed a job with the National Park Service and started a long, distinguished career, much of it spent in Yellowstone, where we met in 1988.

It was her work, in fact, that allowed us to go to Alaska. In the summer of 1998, she was assigned a special public affairs detail in the National Park Service regional office in Anchorage. My own work schedule in Yellowstone was blessedly flexible, so I went along at my own expense. Our time in Brooks Camp, discussed later, was part of a work-related assignment for her, and, again, I paid my own way to join her there.

For Marsha and me it turned out to be a wondrous summer in

the Far North, filled with our shared memories of fabulous landscapes, good times with friends, beautiful salmon streams, a whole new world of bird life and plant communities, and, of course (and at last!), Alaskan bears.

A U.S. Forest Service friend, Henry Shovic, and I drove up to Alaska in advance of Marsha's later arrival by plane, so I got there a week or so before she did. I dropped off Henry at a Forest Service office in Fairbanks, where he had some work to do, and headed south to Denali. There, the National Park Service had a fine system for getting visitors out among the wild animals with the least possible effect on the behavior of the animals and the highest possible odds of the people seeing them without losing any vital organs.

From the park's main entrance, there is an eighty-nine-mile road to the heart of the park, and though always threatened with "improvements," it is mostly unpaved. Anyone may drive the first fifteen miles of this road, a spectacular enough trip, but the rest of it is open only to a system of tour- and shuttle buses that operate on a generously convenient schedule. From these buses visitors of all degrees of familiarity with wild country and wildlife can enjoy the show. If you want to take a hike or just stand by the road and gawk, the driver will let you off wherever you ask (except close to grizzly bears). Do what you like for as long as you like, and when you're ready to leave you just flag down the next bus that comes by.

Though I saw this as a perfectly reasonable way to manage public use in a national park—indeed, I would like it tried in some areas in the Lower 48 parks—I am by temperament a solitary traveler, so I tended to get off the bus and poke around on my own. But when my goal was just to catch a glimpse of as many animals as possible, and just to get a feel for the breadth and reach of this great landscape, the buses were the way to go.

As exhilarating as all this was, I immediately discovered that I had some adjusting to do. The terms of engagement in this kind of wildlife watching took some getting used to, and my first experience of the buses was an almost rude affront to my incautious pride in my hard-earned skills as a wildlife spotter.

The morning of my first bus ride I settled into a front seat in a full bus, recognizing my fifty or so fellow passengers as the usual assortment of park visitors—nice, openly enthusiastic people from all over the world, most of whom had very little experience or interest in serious wildlife watching. As we climbed the grade from park headquarters out onto the taiga, with sensational long-distance views in both directions, I noticed a bull moose way off at the base of the foothills to the south. I said, "There's a moose over there by the hills," loud enough for the driver to hear, which meant that quite a few other people heard too.

The driver had explained that this was how it worked: the whole bus functioned as spotter, and we were all encouraged to sing out whenever we saw something. The driver, an older man with many years' experience on this route, dutifully slowed, while people got their binoculars and cameras aimed. Some left their seats on the other side of the bus to cross the aisle and squeeze in for a look.

When the driver realized how far off the moose was, he announced over his loudspeaker that we would move on and look for something closer. We all settled back down and resumed our watch. After I had done this with two or three remote and barely visible animals, I caught the driver giving me a sidelong half-annoyed "Who *is* this guy?" look, which at first I foolishly thought was flattering. I got cocky, making a flashy over-the-shoulder sighting of a very distant grizzly bear as it climbed through a small patch of bare ground on a high ridge that the bus had already passed. Hardly anyone on the bus could see it up there, and those who could were not necessarily able to tell what it was. It was just a tiny brown blob. But I was so excited to be in Alaska seeing bears, and so pleased that I was good at it, that I couldn't help pointing it out.

But about the time I saw this bear, it began to soak in that I wasn't really helping. After we left the paved road and got onto the less-traveled, unpaved grade, animals were even more common and routinely quite close to the road. For the purposes of the Denali bus, my hard-won spotting skills were not only irrelevant; they were troublesome. I was just showing off.

Worse, I was succumbing to the sort of competitive mood that I always found so distracting among wildlife watchers back home.

35. A Toklat grizzly bear explores the dining opportunities in the Denali tundra. Photo by author.

In any given group of watchers along a road in Yellowstone or Glacier, some people logged their sightings like home runs, eagerly scanning the slopes not merely to see the animal but to see it first. I could feel this urge surfacing, especially when other bus passengers saw something before I did.

So I shut up. There was so much wildlife to be seen, and so many eager eyes trained on the landscape, that little would be missed without my misguided contributions. There were several of Denali's beautiful, near-blonde Toklat grizzly bears—another driver I rode with later advised her passengers to "watch for the little haystacks"—Dall sheep galore, Arctic terns and ptarmigan, the occasional caribou, even a coyote-ish animal that the driver hopefully agreed might be a wolf. It was all an unspeakable thrill for me, but I was, in that one narrow little sense, kind of disappointed. This particular Alaska was a pie in the face of the skills I had been so excited to bring here.

That same pie arrived at an even greater velocity at the next stop on my Alaska bear tour, the famous Brooks Falls in Katmai National Park. Brooks and its wonderful bears rubbed it in some more, making my wildlife-finding skills even more thoroughly irrelevant. At least at Denali I could enjoy the search, scanning the country for wildlife, sorting out all the shades of brown and green, pausing for a while to scan especially promising areas more carefully. By contrast, at Brooks there was no visual search except the one conducted as you walked along the trails, to avoid actually plowing directly into the bears. Wildlife watching is almost incomprehensibly different without the thrill of the chase but, I learned, can be no less thrilling for that.

14

Brooks Bears

I first heard about the Brooks River, and about Alaska's other famous bear-viewing areas, more than twenty years earlier when I started writing bear books. Eventually, the extraordinary situations under which people were enjoying Alaskan brown bears became a kind of implausible truth I mentally held off to the side of more conventional knowledge. I knew all this was happening, but knowing so was only some pleasant and marginally imaginable intellectual freight until I saw it for myself.

I read and heard most about the tremendous congregations of coastal brown bears at McNeil River, located in a state-run sanctuary on the east coast of the Alaskan peninsula just north of Katmai National Park, but I gradually realized that many of the most startling photographs I saw published were from Brooks Falls. It was here, for example, that the renowned nature photographer Thomas Mangelsen took his exquisitely timed photograph (published, among other places, on the cover of his gorgeous book *Images of Nature*) of a large brown bear leaning out from the lip of a waterfall, his mouth wide open and about to receive a chrome-bright salmon, caught broadside in mid-leap, its head just inches from the bear's teeth.

As a longtime observer of bear management, I found even our arrival in the park fascinating. Almost all visitors arrive at Brooks Camp by float plane, from which a ranger immediately ushers them into a cabin-size visitor center right by the shore and gives them the most intensive bear-safety training session I'd ever seen. Mar-

36. From the slopes of Dumpling Mountain, northwest of Brooks Camp, you can see the whole length of Brooks River, which flows west across the isthmus from Brooks Lake (*on right*) to Naknek Lake. Brooks Falls, not visible in the photo, is roughly in the middle of the isthmus. The visitor facilities at Brooks Camp are along the lake shore just below the outlet of the river. To the south and southeast the great wilderness of Katmai National Park stretches off into the distance. Photo by author.

37. From the same vantage point of the Brooks River on Dumpling Mountain, but zooming in on the river's outlet, the old pontoon bridge—since replaced by a more permanent structure—is visible, as are some of the buildings of Brooks Camp. Fly fishers and bears share, often quite anxiously, the final few bends and pools of the river near the bridge. Photo by author.

sha and I, and our fellow passengers, sat down and were treated to a terrific professional presentation full of the specifics of getting along with bears at this remarkable place.

I understand there have been some significant changes since we were there, so what follows is the tale of our visit, more than twenty years ago now. Brooks Camp was made up of the lodge for guests and a variety of employee housing and other necessary facilities on both sides of the Brooks River. The falls, where the bears most famously concentrate, are a fair walk from the lodge, but the bears are in fact free to roam wherever they want in the whole area.

The advice was thoughtfully but very firmly given: Don't even *think* about carrying food around with you; it goes in the high cache (a miniature log cabin on log stilts, with a ladder up to its little door) just across the trail from the visitor center. This includes the candy bars in your pockets; *all* food stays here. If you're hungry, get your food bag from the cache and eat right there, at the picnic tables next to the cache.

Make noise wherever you go, so you never surprise a bear. Clap, sing, talk, the more noise the better. Clap some more. Then clap. Stay at least fifty yards from any bear, and if it's a sow with cubs make it a hundred yards. Right outside the visitor center, there's a little sign on a tree that will tell you that you're exactly fifty yards from the life-size, brown-painted wooden bear silhouette you can see down the trail by the ranger station. This will give you some idea of how far fifty yards is and how big a bear looks at that distance.

When you catch a salmon you want to keep (I perked up here because catching was made to seem like a probability if not a certainty), you must immediately stop fishing, put the fish in one of the plastic bags provided, and hurry it to the ice house for storage. No lingering to show it off and brag, and especially no streamside gutting and cleaning of the fish; *go right now.* If you are playing a fish and a bear comes by, break the line; don't risk feeding that fish to the bear, who will thus learn to approach other fishermen for similar rewards. If you surprise a bear on a trail, don't run. Talk reassuringly, wave your arms, clap your hands, back away slowly.

38. From the viewing platform at the mouth of Brooks River park staff routinely informed the fishermen of the near approach of the bears, with whom they shared the salmon, at which time the fishermen vacated the water to await developments. The south end of the pontoon bridge is visible on the right. Photo by author.

The trail south from the lodge stays near the lakeshore, passes the small store, the fish-storage shack, and another outbuilding or two, then emerges from under the low forest canopy at the north shore of Brooks River, right where that stream meets the lake. A narrow, softly bobbing pontoon bridge (this has since been replaced with something more permanent) with a sturdy pipe railing on both sides crosses the river just upstream from its wide mouth, where it flows into Naknek Lake. By this point in our visit I was nearly frantic to see one of the legendary Brooks bears, but none were in sight.

Across the way, where the bridge touched the south shore of the river, there was a long, elevated wooden platform from which park staff and visitors watched for the putative bears. The platform was a revelation to me. Partly obscured by small trees, fronting the shore of the river just where it broadens and transforms itself from a flow to a bay, the platform was a long, dog-legged wooden affair with stairs on one end and a handicap-access ramp on the other, both leading up to the railed viewing area about ten feet above the ground. Both the stairs and the ramp were gated with simple wooden gates such as you would expect at the front of any fenced yard. I was beginning to sense the differences between this place and my home more keenly now. It was obvious that the elevated wooden platform was regarded as a sanctuary for people. And unless the local rangers were using magic bear-warding spells on those flimsy gates, the only imaginable explanation for this improbable arrangement was that the stern anti-food discipline enforced on park visitors was almost perfectly successful. Any bear who wanted to go up there on the platform and look around was not going to be stopped by the gates, so no bear must ever want to.

Beside the platform, there was the start of a gravel road that headed back into the forest on a course more or less parallel with the south side of the river. After a few hundred yards we came to a trail that led off into the mottled shade of the spruce forest on the right, back toward the river.

On the trail, the leader of our little group was Bill Pierce, superintendent of the park. He immediately established himself as the kind of person with whom I most like to hike in bear country— specifically, one who doesn't want to surprise a bear. With vigilant regularity, his conversations were punctuated by sharp handclaps like small-caliber gunshots, and his frequent calls to the bears boomed and echoed in the woods. To this authoritative accompaniment, we wound through a flat forested bottomland, a still, low-elevation white spruce forest with a mixture of familiar and unfamiliar undergrowth that was broken with unnerving frequency by cross-trails that were created and maintained entirely by the bears that I still knew only as large, omnivorous allegations.

Leaving the spruce forest behind, we climbed and walked along a low, hummocky ridge in a sparse birch wood. A ranger later told us that because of the local density of roaming bears the ridge was known informally as "Scary Hill." As the trail descended from the sunny top of Scary Hill it reentered the birch-alder-willow forest that solidly walled both sides of the stream. When still well back from the river, and perhaps fifteen feet above the river's level, the trail ended at another wooden gate, this one featuring a simple sign with the international symbol prohibiting something—the red circle with diagonal slash—in this case bears. Behind the diag-

39. The "No Bears" symbol at the entrance gate to the Brooks Falls viewing platform. Photo by author.

onal slash was a very official looking silhouette of a bear: *No bears allowed*. This seemed amusing almost to the point of hysteria right then and gave the whole place a fine and slightly desperate comic relief that I would later realize characterized much of the relationship between people and bears at this astounding place. (There is now a third formally constituted viewing area, a platform overlooking a riffled reach of the river not far downstream from the falls.)

Opening the gate, Bill led us along a level ramp, underneath which the slope fell away, until we reached the main viewing platform, a two-level affair that would hold a tightly packed forty standing people. There were about twenty there, all looking out over the river, which at this point was about one hundred and fifty feet wide, and at the falls, which were about seven feet high. The river flowed into view from the left, dropped over the falls, and continued on down to the right through a long islanded riffle. The water was visible for hundreds of yards downstream, then it bent out of sight into its last curves before flowing under the pontoon bridge and out into Naknek Lake. I only took in these peripheral features later, because there were bears at the falls. *There they are!*

These were bears writ large; after a summer of feeding on salmon the males often reach one thousand pounds in weight and the females six hundred or more—essentially twice the weight of my grizzly bears back home. The nearest one, about a third of the way across toward the other side of the falls, was unquestionably posed in the exact spot where Mangelsen's famous bear-salmon scene had taken place. Another was just a few feet beyond him, like a second image in a mirror. A third was standing in the river closer to the far shore, perhaps ten feet out from the base of the falling water, staring intently at the foam. Nobody moved; they just stared and waited. Occasionally a big head swung slowly to one side or the other, or a hefty paw would shift to brace itself better against the current.

After a few moments I noticed that their heads seemed differently proportioned than those of the bears I knew: longer and more angular perhaps. Their ears seemed more pronounced as well. Though neglected by most of the writers who have commented on why bears reach so successfully into so many corners of the human

40. The extraordinary, world-famous, and profusely photographed view from the Brooks Falls platform. Photo by author.

imagination, bear ears are an important part of what makes the animal so appealing. Imagine how different the bear would look to us, and how different would be our reaction to the sight of it, if its ears were pointed like a fox's, or droopy like a hound's. Those little rounded ears, with their almost tacked-on presentation well back on the head, have contributed greatly to the bear's enormous range of imagined personalities in human culture. Small and neutral enough in shape to be cute when we needed cuteness, the ears were inconsequential when fury was called for. Try to imagine a cottontail rabbit with its eyes aflame with rage and its lips drawn back in a vicious snarl; even if you succeed in imagining the rage and the snarl, the big perky ears will ruin the effect.

Brooks bears, at least these big males that dominated the best spots at the falls, brought something new to the whole ear issue. Once noticed, it distracted me all week. For the size of the animal I doubt that their ears were out of proportion, but through some combination of color and shape they were immediately more noticeable. The bear ear is not a flat flap; it curls around the ear opening. Perhaps because they sometimes seemed a few shades lighter in color than the head, and because that lighter shade caught the light so well (on sunny days they were almost bright), they became an added attraction in my enjoyment of the animal. They looked like big furry softballs glued on there. They were irredeemably cute.

15

Waiting

B rooks Falls is not straight. It does not break over an even, unbending shelf that runs directly from one bank of the Brooks River to the other. Instead, the brink is curvilinear; it swerves forward and back a couple times on its way across the river. In some places, big dark rocks protrude from the brink, or poke through the falls themselves. But almost all the way across, the brink itself is abrupt; the water rushes over the ragged, rocky edge with a rim of smooth blue-green flow that tumbles down into the white of the fall. The pool below the falls is a frothy turmoil of foam and rock, the water roiling around submerged obstacles and churning along for some distance before reorganizing itself into a relatively flat, dark flow and continuing on downstream.

Over the ages, the salmon who run up this stream have found their way to the best holding water below the falls, places that provide them sufficient depth and "traction" to make the furious short burst of speed that will carry them up to the river above.

Over the same ages, the bears have identified with great precision the very best places to stand to intercept those flights. There they stand, knee- or chest-deep in the powerful flow, and there they wait. They have also identified the best places in the foamy turbulence below the falls to watch for fish swimming by. Those bears who can't take and defend the best places on the brink settle for these. Other bears, too low in the hierarchy to earn any of these places, cruise the edges of the stream, or adopt more creative strategies that I was to witness as the week went on. But for all the bears who were seri-

41. Brooks Falls bears at work. Photo by author.

42. Patience rewarded: a sockeye salmon has jumped directly into the mouth of a waiting bear. Photo by author.

ous contenders for the good places, it was a matter of getting into position, concentrating on the source of the salmon, and waiting.

And waiting. We arrived very early in the summer run, so fish numbers would have been fairly low anyway, but the year of our visit was also the second consecutive season in which the Bristol Bay sockeye salmon run was judged a disaster. For whatever combination of reasons, the sockeyes were returning in extremely low numbers, which meant that the bears—and those of us watching—were waiting a long time between fish. Sometimes ten or even fifteen minutes would pass before a fish would rocket out of the foam, and either flop into the upper part of the falls to be washed back down, make it into the upper river, or meet the lunge of a waiting bear, who often missed. If the bear caught the fish, he immediately vacated his spot and took his prize to shore to eat it. Depending upon some unclear interpersonal dynamic that prevailed that day, another bear might or might not try to occupy the empty spot while he was gone.

The overriding biological truth of this scene, the thing that ruled the behavior and thus the excitement of all the bears and humans up and down the river, was that nothing happens unless salmon are there. The more salmon, the more happens. Many salmon, and more happens than can be comprehended.

My favorite description of this falls when the salmon were at their thickest is probably the first detailed account of the event in print. It was left by Robert Griggs, the National Geographic Society–sponsored scientist whose series of exploratory expeditions into the Katmai country between 1915 and 1917 led to the creation of Katmai National Monument in 1918. In 1919, his group camped at Brooks River and witnessed what was probably the peak of the run in a good year:

> Here we stood for hours, held by the fascination of one of the most wonderful sights afforded by the animal kingdom, as the endless procession of fish kept leaping high in the air, up and over the falls.
>
> Never did a second elapse between jumps. Sometimes as many as six fish were in the air at once. The jump appeared to require their full powers; none made the attempt except at the lowest notch in the falls, and none jumped clear over in a way to suggest that they could have gone

43. The source of the spectacle: sockeye salmon, typically about two feet long, attract and hold the attention of photographers, general visitors, anglers, and bears throughout the season of their spawning run. Photo by author.

much higher if necessary. Many of the leaps were so wide of the mark as to give the impression that they were not serious attempts, but rather in the nature of reconnaissances—efforts to learn the best place for the ascent. Often the fish struck themselves on the sharp rocks. Among those below the falls were many terribly lacerated by such accidents—so far gone that there was little probability of their ever succeeding in the leap.

At first we were inclined to think that very few were successful, but careful observation showed that great numbers were getting up. After a number of counts at different times, we estimated that they were ascending at the rate of about 20 a minute, or 1,200 an hour.

Success in watching or appreciating wildlife is not simply measurable. As I'd been so forcefully reminded at Denali, part of the challenge is in coming to terms with how differently the game is played from one place to the next. Standing there at Brooks Falls I was in a kind of charmed awe. It was enough for me to have these unmoving bears in view and to enjoy the quality of their attention: that pure, guileless physical and mental alertness of animals at ease in their environment. But as I watched and wondered, I was also struck by the quality of my own attention and the deceptive simplicity of the scene.

44. Bears move easily through the familiar waters around and above the falls. Photo by author.

We have always loved the charismatic herbivorous megafauna—deer, elk, moose, bison, caribou, and so on—and nowadays we, at least many of us, have also come to adore the equally charismatic predators. Brooks Falls makes it so easy to enjoy all this simplemindedly because we get to see a kind of predation that evokes little or no empathy with the prey. After all, they're "just fish." At Brooks we are usually spared the harder sights of these same bears at different seasons, calmly dismantling a still-bleating caribou calf, or rousting and hastily inhaling a whole family of squirrels. Brooks is in that way ideal for the beginning wildlife watcher because it offers such quick rewards; it gets you hooked on the whole business of observing. Thus it also eases you into the activity without any warning of the harder emotional dues you will pay if you stay for a while and take in all the things that are really going on. The sound of the cracking, popping backbone of salmon being fed on by a nearby bear is an early warning of the real show, and of the aesthetic and even spiritual challenges ahead of you if you accept that animals are best appreciated on their own terms, no matter how dramatically those terms may differ from ours.

16

Back to Scary Hill

O ne morning at Brooks Marsha and I reached the trail-head a little before 11:00 a.m., and dutifully clapped and shouted our way through the spruce forest, then up onto Scary Hill and along its winding, lumpy path through the birches. We made noise the whole way; the people on the platform could surely hear us coming.

I was in front as we came down off Scary Hill. The little gate with its "no bears allowed" sign was directly ahead of us when I unexpectedly stepped into an old Jimmy Buffett song, words to the effect of "That's when I first saw the bear; he was a big Kodiak-lookin' feller, about nineteen feet tall." Sure enough, under the shady canopy of an old birch just to the right of the gate, one of the big, light-brown bears was standing broadside to us, watching us approach. Later examination of the spot suggested that we were perhaps fifty feet from him right then. Maybe it was more. It seemed a good bit less.

In my years of wandering in bear country in the Lower 48, I have seen a fair number of bears at various distances in the back-country, and even surprised some that immediately ran off, but I had never found myself face-to-face with one, nothing between us but air, this close. Neither had Marsha. As I've said before, over those years, I had plenty of time to think about what I would do when this finally happened. I read hugely in both the scientific and the popular literatures on bear encounters. I talked to experts, as well as to people who had had such encounters and walked away, and even to mauling victims. I absorbed all the advice, considered the odds of each possible tactic working or failing, and developed such habits as could be cultivated, such as being especially careful near noisy streams, in tight corners among rocks or trees, and on windy days when my own noise might be blown away. I tried always to keep an eye out not just for bears but for tracks, scat, diggings, and big, climbable trees.

But I knew that no amount of planning provided reasonable assurance that when I did meet a bear up close my personal reaction would be the right one, or even a sensible one. This isn't because the advice I received and all the learning I did wasn't essential or because good bear-country habits aren't worth developing. It is because inside each of us is a different person that we don't know very well, and that person is just waiting to come out and surprise us with some strange combination of fright, fortitude, common sense, and idiocy when it is finally our turn to meet the bear.

When it finally happened there at Scary Hill, my reaction was, sad to say, more prosaic than educated. Briefly and softly, yet sincerely, I swore. It was entirely involuntary, no thought or creative phrasing involved. I just said, "Oh shit." This caused Marsha to glance up from the rough trail's uneven footing, look past my shoulder, and see the bear, too, but her reaction was more restrained and less profane.

The bear, by contrast, showed no reaction at all. It didn't ruffle a bit of its half-acre of furry muscle or even twitch a cute ear.

We stood there only a few seconds before I said, "Let's just walk back." We turned around and moved back up the trail onto Scary Hill, just far enough so that the bear was no longer in sight. There we hesitated, doing as good a job of milling around uncertainly as two people could. We had not seen the bear move the whole time it was in view. After a bit of calling back and forth with the ranger on the platform, who had seen us approach and told us that the bear had now settled down and gotten comfy right on the trail, we went back to the bridge.

In Yellowstone or Glacier, this close an encounter could easily have been a matter of the most dire peril. Such a short distance

45. The bears regularly walked directly past the falls viewing platform, providing landscape-scale views of their massive backs. Photo by author.

was well inside the "fight or flight" reaction threshold of most of our larger wild animals down here, especially in the backcountry (animals that calmly graze while surrounded by camera-faced tourists along a park road will often flee from the very sound of approaching hikers the next day a mile from the same road). All my book-learning on grizzly bears suggested to me that at that instant when "I first saw the bear" I was his, and he very possibly would claim ownership. Despite my best efforts to follow the rules, I had messed up (blaming the bear is nonsense), and I was toast if the bear wanted to bother with me. So was Marsha.

But my more recent learning about Alaskan brown bears seemed to teach me different. Encounters like ours, and considerably closer ones, were an everyday occurrence at Brooks. People and bears bounced off each other's personal spaces constantly, ricocheting around like a flock of finches at a feeder with too few perches. I would have more such encounters with *Ursus arctos* in the next few days than I had had in the Lower 48 in the previous twenty-five years.

Before I went to Alaska, a biologist friend with Alaskan research experience told me, "That's a different bear up there. It's much more mellow and easygoing." The rationale for this was that these bears were so fat and happy from the ever-flowing larder of the river, and had spent so many hundreds of generations living this good life, that they were a lot harder to alarm.

Even though I could absorb this information on an intellectual level, I never stopped having trouble with it on an emotional level. My conditioning was too strong.

Besides, I knew too much about bears. The bears at Brooks emerged from their dens long before the salmon started running. Until there were fish to eat, they had to make their living eating other things, many of which were warm-blooded animals that would try to run away. These big bears, as lumbering and benign as they might seem, were no strangers to working hard to acquire prey. They ate any animal they could get. They might behave differently at the falls than they did at other seasons and in other places—but they were still bears.

But let's back up here for a moment, to that critical moment as we came down Scary Hill into view of the gate and the bear. Yes, we did indeed ignore all advice to the contrary and turn our backs to the bear and walk away—not our finest moment as experienced bear-country travelers, but there it was. My only excuse—which I admit falls well short of being an actual thought-out reason—is that we were in unfamiliar territory and none of this seemed all that real; frightening, yes, but in an oddly abstract sort of way. These bears were behaving as I'd been warned they would, and were in the process of giving me the feeling that I'd wandered into some parallel bear universe where nothing I'd been taught in the Lower 48 was valid.

Besides, as wrong as I may have been in my impression at the time, I have to say that for all its hugeness, that particular bear was in no discernible way threatening us. There were none of the signs one might expect if a bear was surprised or agitated. I don't claim to be any great shakes at reading a bear's posture or mood, but that bear really did seem to be looking at us—as it probably had looked at hundreds of other blithely meandering humans—

with only the most casual of interest, as in, "Hmm, there's a couple tourists; this'll be good."

On the other hand, none of the above is to imply that Marsha and I weren't really scared right then. We were quite ready to believe that if that bear had stood up on its hind legs, it would indeed have been about nineteen feet tall.

17

Grizzly Dreams

E very now and then since I started spending time in grizzly
bear country I have a dream about bears. This isn't something that obsesses me or rules my sleep, and I am only
aware of it happening maybe a couple times a year. But the dreams
are usually of that most vivid and compelling type that linger in my
mind almost like real memories, especially for that first day or so
after I wake up. They're hard to shake off, and I can still recite especially exciting moments from several of these dream adventures.

They are never nightmares. I have yet to be chased by a bear
in these dreams, and no blood has ever been shed. But they are
always deeply uneasy experiences, without exception characterized by close encounters between me and very large grizzly bears
who have complete access to me. These bears may be wandering
around quite calmly in my house while I wait more or less cor-
nered in some room with no way out except past them. The bears
aren't intentionally hunting me, but they're almost certain to find
me soon. In other dreams, occurring out on the landscape, the
bears may be as thick as sheep on a hillside while I walk a winding road through the middle of them. Once or twice the landscape
has slipped over into a fantastic, Tolkienesque setting of perfectly
round trees and rolling hills of storybook tidiness; then the bears
were almost cartoonlike, but still looming and ominous for all
their cuddly caricature.

The experience of avoiding bears is something all of us who hike
near them know about. We know the heightening of attention, the

urgent alertness, the suspenseful possibilities. We spend our time, day after day, hopefully waiting for nothing to go wrong. I assume that my dreams are an extension of that exercise, in which I bring the source of the fear out in the open. The bears in those dreams don't quite threaten—they never growl or snarl—but they impend so heavily that I am no longer appreciating their very existence as I routinely do when hiking. In the dreams I am just waiting, and without exception the bears are there and I have no escape from them if they choose to approach or attack. It isn't the likelihood of attack that makes these dreams so stirring; it is the suspense, and the abject vulnerability.

Because of all this, I recognized Brooks Camp. It embodied my dreams. There were large stretches of forest, trail, and riverside where I stood in perfect vulnerability. Certainly the little "safe zones," such as the platforms with their charming "no bears" signs, provided no sure sanctuary. The little cabin we shared with some locals during our stay had an enormous kitchen window, a simple set of lightly framed panes of glass that the two biggest bears in Katmai could have stepped through side by side. Along the local trails, there were trees all over the place, some quite climbable, but at any moment when I might look around, very few of the trees within range seemed stout enough to withstand one of these big bears if it really wanted to get me out of it. For a week, there was no escape.

I have wondered, if I were to spend a whole summer at Brooks, living and working there, moving around the trails and among the bears, would I get used to it and finally come to a new set of terms with the whole idea of wild bears? Wouldn't I owe it to myself and to the bears to make that temperamental adjustment? Probably so, but I'm not sure I could manage it.

FOUR

The Literary Bear

18

Bear Books

A wise fisherman once wrote that "some of the best fishing is done not in water but in print," an eloquent bow to all the happy adventuring we anglers do—not on the stream but while sitting at home reading one of the inexhaustible supply of books that have been published on the subject. If you've gotten this far into my book, you probably are inclined to agree that the same thing is true of enjoying, learning about, and generally sharing the world of bears. Reading about bears is fine consolation for when you can't actually be out there in bear country, and it's a great joy in its own right.

I don't doubt that for all the time I've spent out on the trails in bear country I've spent much more time at home or in some library reading about them (for a bit of contrast, I will confess that while I have been known to carry a portable edition of Walton's *Compleat Angler* or some other classic work of angling lore in the back pocket of my fishing vest, I've never yet carried any of my favorite bear books with me on the trail).

So in the next few chapters I offer a kind of navigational guide— and a sampling of countless adventures—in the form of a list with commentary, through the world of vintage bear reading. I won't go so far as to call all or even most of these books classics, because some are included for reasons other than the authority of their information or the elegance of their prose. But I'm sure that an acquaintance with the books included here should give you a fair handle on how we've described and imagined bears over the past couple centuries. The list is nothing like exhaustive, but it's a good start.

Just as the real mother lode of bear science will always be found in scientific journals, technical papers, monographs, management reports, and conference proceedings, the real mother lode of less formal thinking about bears is in the much, much larger volume of popularly written material in articles and books. As I mentioned in chapter 8, in the early 1970s, when I began my exploration of all that informal material, I read and enjoyed the shorter items by the hundreds, but I've always had a soft spot for books, with their greater room for detail and the peculiar if often illusory sense of completeness that their embracing covers implied.

When I began, there weren't all that many bear books to be had without considerable effort, which was a good thing considering my intermittent ranger salary and the even more modest university subsistence stipend paid out during my occasional inconclusive bouts of graduate school. But forty or fifty years ago, when acquiring an out-of-print book was a treasure hunt and books were patiently tracked down either by resorting to a few antiquarian natural history catalogs or, more often, by dusty foraging in used bookstores, I discovered each "new" old book with the excitement of a gold prospector. At first I knew so little about what I was looking for that the discovery of even an important bear book's existence sometimes coincided with my first sight of it on a bookstore shelf.

Among my hopes for the following list is that it will to some extent save you from having to go through the same hit-or-miss discovery of the older literature as I did. On the other hand, I don't mind also saying that I wouldn't trade that drawn-out research experience for something easier if I could. It was high bibliographical adventure.

I have chosen to confine the following list to what I am casually calling "vintage" books. To further heighten the egregious subjectivity of such a decision, I have settled on a cut-off date of 1967, for several reasons, none better than that date allows me to conclude the list with Andy Russell's *Grizzly Country*, a literary mile-

46. A bear lover's bookshelf of vintage and modern classics. **Photo by** author.

stone if ever there was one. Besides its stirring personal narrative about Russell's own many wilderness adventures, *Grizzly Country* also contains his thoughtful and well-informed distillation of so much bear lore and literature up to his time. For extra credit, Russell's book also serves beautifully, perhaps even uniquely, as both a cause and a symbol of our modern awakening to the value of bears to society and the urgent need to take better care of them and their wild world than we have so far. These were all good reasons for me to bookend the modern end of the shelf with *Grizzly Country.*

The list is, alas, also confined to English-language books. I know that many other cultures and nations also enjoy literary traditions rich in bear science and lore. I wish I could read it all, and I ardently hope for translations of quite a few such books, but I doubt I will get that far. Perhaps you will.

The list is arranged chronologically by the date of each book's first appearance and then grouped in chapters that loosely and imprecisely locate them in a bit more specific historical context. Such structure, though admittedly artificial, appeals to my historian's need for a simple sequential order, but listing them thus also provides a kind of metanarrative—a satisfyingly snooty literary term I never imagined using until just now—of how, over the years, these accumulating books have both shaped and reflected our evolving perspective on bears. Besides, in deciding how to organize a list this informal and comparatively brief, I am skeptical of any other imaginable topical grouping—for example, by region, by species, by hunting versus natural history versus fiction, and so on—that I am pretty sure would end up feeling forced, with this or that title shoehorned under some heading that doesn't really do it justice. Chronology is cleanest.

I present the list with no pretense that it is definitive even for the time period covered by it, but I do hope it is representative. Some of these books are indeed recognized as milestones, others are essentially unknown or forgotten beyond the small circle of the most determined bear enthusiasts. Some are trustworthy, others are suspect even on a good day. I chose them from a larger body of bear books for those very characteristics and also because, for reasons that I probably couldn't fully explain even if I tried, they just appeal to me and seem to belong here.

The three most neglected categories in this list are hunting books, children's books, and fiction, all three of which exist in great numbers, far too many to include here. Quite a few of the books in the list do involve hunting, sometimes even to the exclusion of everything else; how could such a list not include them, considering for how long killing bears was our primary way of relating to them? The small number of children's books I've included struck me either as especially important in their own right or just as well-told bear stories. There are, of course, quite a few especially fine bear-related stories and novels, too, but as with the hunting and children's books, they would require a long list of their own to adequately illustrate the qualities, difficulties, and disappointments of their subgenre. I hereby invite those among you who might be so inclined to consider that a study of the bear in fiction is a subject worthy of one or more books that still need to be written.

I must also add a note of caution. Here and there in these books you are sure to come upon displays of values we now rightly find troubling or downright abhorrent, certainly about bears and nature, but also about gender, race, and other matters to which our ancestors were more poorly attuned than we like to hope we are today. By recommending these books to your attention I am not endorsing those views or any other outdated assertions, opinions, or attitudes expressed therein. These books are reflections of their authors' lives and times. It does us no harm, and almost certainly a lot of good, to be reminded of how things were. And there is great comfort in knowing, among other encouraging things, that although practically all of the books included in the following chapters were written by white males, those guys are no longer the only ones studying and writing about bears today.

Enough with explaining. I'm confident that this is just the sort of list that will introduce you to the joys of bear lore and science as they were before the great flowering of bear books that has occurred during the past half century. How I wish a list like this had been available when I began my own exploration of bear literature.

Where you take your reading from here is up to you, of course, but be assured there is much, much more awaiting your attention and enjoyment.

19

Trailblazers

We begin with some pioneers. The authors and books discussed in this chapter were by no means the first to encounter the bear species they describe, but they were among the first to leave us full chronicles of so many of their encounters. And though tall tales about bears are a common part of bear lore from much older days than are recounted here, some of these authors were important pioneers in turning the bear into vividly portrayed characters in books of fiction.

1804–1806

Meriwether Lewis, William Clark, Charles Floyd, Patrick Gass, John Ordway, and Joseph Whitehouse

No member of the great Corps of Discovery wrote a book dedicated entirely to bears, but I cannot *not* begin my list with Lewis, Clark, and the other members of their expedition, whose combined journals provide us with a uniquely important body of pioneering writing about bears, especially the grizzly bears that were at that time almost completely unknown to European Americans. Though Lewis and Clark were preceded in their sightings and reports of grizzly bears by other European American explorers—in Canada, on the West Coast, and for all we know elsewhere in the mountain West and Southwest—the Corps journalists' descriptions of the bears and chronicles of their adventures with them still may be the single greatest shaper of the modern idea of the grizzly bear.

47. The journals of the Lewis and Clark expedition gave almost all readers their first and, for much of the nineteenth and twentieth centuries, most opinion-forming look at the grizzly bear. This engraving, entitled *An American having struck a Bear but not killed him, escapes into a Tree*, appeared repeatedly and in various forms in the published journal of expedition member Patrick Gass, first published in 1807. The artist almost certainly had never seen a grizzly bear, portraying it here in dog-like form and in later editions in more piglike renditions. The man, Private Hugh McNeal, having surprised the bear at close quarters, was thrown from his horse, seen here running off. McNeal managed to club the bear with his "musquet," but the bear quickly recovered and treed McNeal, who wisely waited three hours in the tree to ensure that the bear had really left the area.

For the full, in-context, firsthand accounts left by these men, you can do no better than refer to Gary Moulton's monumental thirteen-volume edition of their journals (published by the University of Nebraska Press, 1983–2001), which handsomely displaces several earlier but also worthy editions of the journals dating well back into the early 1800s. If you want to read just one tasty volume of Moulton's that is especially blessed in grizzly bear encounters, try volume 4 (published in 1987), which contains the expedition leaders' journals from April 7 to July 27, 1895, covering their travels from the Mandan Villages in present-day North Dakota to the Three Forks of the Missouri River in present-day Montana. In fact, there's no better way to get acquainted with the pace, feel, and essential landscape of their bear experiences than by reading that whole volume.

Among the many points of interest in this exciting material are the inevitable early stirrings and vexations of taxonomy—the Corps' attempts, like many before them around the world, to sort out just how many different species of bears they encountered. Matters of color, size, anatomical specifics, and behavior all figured in the Corps' halting attempts to come to terms with so many sizes, shades, and personalities of bears along their route. Their discussions of these taxonomic puzzles anticipate similar ones by many later writers, some of whom we'll hear more about later.

I would be remiss if I didn't at least alert you to my *Lewis and Clark Among the Grizzlies*, which includes in full all journal accounts of grizzly bears by all members of the Corps with substantial additional commentary. (Don't give me any guff about self-promotion here—I'm just trying to be helpful, and it's the only thorough book on the subject. You can take my word for it that by mentioning it here I'm not opening floodgates of excessive royalties.)

While I'm at it, here's another post–1967 book I had better recommend. The grizzly bear adventures of Lewis and Clark were continued in abundance by the traders, trappers, and other "mountain men" who arrived in the Rocky Mountains hot on the heels of the Corps of Discovery. Though none of them wrote a whole book about the bears, either, many of them did record their exciting and sometimes terrible experiences with them. A splendid compilation of those shorter accounts is Fred R. Gowans, *Mountain Man and Grizzly*.

1860

Theodore Henry Hittell on Grizzly Adams

Grizzly Adams, who is commonly remembered as James Capen Adams but whose real name seems to have been John rather than James, did not a write a book, but his story was professionally chronicled by San Francisco historian-journalist Theodore Hittell, who interviewed him extensively when Adams was maintaining a famous zoo in the city in the late 1850s. Hittell's book,

48. Grizzly Adams, a memorable portrait from Theodore Hittell's *Adventures of James Capen Adams* (1860).

The Adventures of James Capen Adams, Mountaineer and Grizzly Bear Hunter of California, did more than any other publication to ensure the survival not merely of Adams's fame but of a wealth of adventure stories and some intriguing natural history as well. Just don't expect the Grizzly Adams that Hittell wrote about to act or sound very much like the guy on the television show.

Adams did, however, lead an extraordinary life during his years in the western wilderness, not only as a bear hunter but as a bear tamer and, occasionally, as a companion and trusted friend of bears of his close acquaintance. His accounts of life in the western American wilderness are of interest as verbal snapshots of a world now long lost to us.

Having offered those sincere and enthusiastic endorsements, I can add that Hittell's text contains a fair number of problematic passages having to do with natural history and the geography of his travels. However, I am happy to say that this provides me an opportunity to recommend Susan Snyder's gorgeously illustrated and exhaustively researched anthology *Bear in Mind: The California Grizzly*. Among the grand array of early California bear material in her book, Snyder reprints a letter that no less a California wilderness authority than John Muir wrote to Hittell in 1899. It appears that Hittell had contacted Muir for advice about publishing a new edition of *The Adventures of James Capen Adams*. Muir's response was both encouraging and blunt, as he pointed out that there were "so many errors the book has an unreal air." Hittell apparently took Muir's specific suggestions seriously, because when a new edition did appear, in 1911, at least some of the errors had been corrected.

Important modern considerations of Adams's career are provided by California historical scholar Richard Dillon in *The Legend of Grizzly Adams: California's Greatest Mountain Man* and by zoologists-turned-historians Tracy Storer and Lloyd Tevis, in *California Grizzly*.

1860

Thomas Mayne Reid

Mayne Reid's novel *Bruin: The Grand Bear Hunt* goes to show what you may find, no matter how specialized or narrow your field of interest, if you explore the older, darker corners of long-forgotten nature lore and adventure literature—and all the better if you are adept at conducting such explorations on the internet.

Reid was an Irish-born adventurer, teacher, occasional soldier, and prodigiously productive novelist, whose juvenile and adult novels were set in the many places he traveled and well beyond. According to something I found online, Edgar Allan Poe, who used to drink with Reid during the latter's time in the United States, said that he was "a colossal but most picturesque liar. He fibs on a surprising scale but with the finish of an artist, and that is why I listen to him attentively." If Poe really said that, and if it was true, perhaps Reid found his gift for lying a useful skill in producing such a sustained torrent of long, involved, and picturesque novels.

Bruin is about a pair of wealthy Russian brothers whose father, the Baron Grodonoff, was so obsessed with bears that he sends his sons on a global hunting adventure to collect (that is, kill and return with) specimens of every type of bear in the world. The plot, whatever its other successes or failures may be, was almost certainly the first such extended literary tour of all of the world's then known bear country. Whatever I might have thought of the story itself, it was more than worth reading just for this travelogue.

Today *Bruin* reminds us that the middle of the nineteenth century was an exciting time in bear science. As one of the brothers points out to the other, partway through their adventure, "It should be remembered that it is only a few years since the bears of the Himalayas, of the Great Andes of America, and those of the East-Indian islands—and even the bear of Mount Lebanon—became known to the scientific world."

This was an important assertion. Whatever factual errors we might notice in *Bruin*, we have to admit that, among all his other interests, Reid did find his way to much of the latest news from the world of bear science. His narrative also showcases the even then unstable state of bear species classification (his young hunters missed only the giant panda, then still virtually unknown outside of China and not until much later firmly declared to be a real bear), which is still being fine-tuned 160 years later.

Reid is generally forgotten now, proof that mere high-volume production does not guarantee literary immortality. But notable individuals as diverse as Theodore Roosevelt, Anton Chekhov,

49. The adventuresome frontispiece from Thomas Mayne Reid's *Bruin* (1860).

Arthur Conan Doyle, and Vladimir Nabokov are among the count-less people whose boyhoods and literary ambitions are known to have been enriched by his tales. I've read some of his other adven-ture novels and their appeal is obvious; exciting things hardly ever stop happening.

1900

Ernest Thompson Seton

Seton's *The Biography of a Grizzly* is the compelling fictional story of a Yellowstone-area bear cub named Wahb who grows into a huge, man-wise, and dreaded ruler of a vast and wild mountain domain. The book must certainly be among the all-time, best-selling works of bear-related fiction (but see also Winnie-the-Pooh).

To the modern eye it looks and reads like a profusely illustrated children's book, which I suppose it was when published, but it plainly was and still is also enjoyed by adults. Though he went on to great achievement and acclaim as a naturalist, Seton's writings and illustrations, especially those from early in his career, when he published the *Biography*, were criticized for their anthropomor-phic treatment of many animals. The *Biography* is undeniably full of heartfelt depictions of very people-like bears.

Not that I mind, really; whether one is troubled by his par-ticular brand of anthropomorphism may have more to do with one's own predilections than with Seton's reliability either as a storyteller or as a naturalist. His bears do occasionally exhibit behavior beyond what modern science might give them credit for, but those episodes are balanced to a great extent by his many small accuracies about the then little-known lives of real bears. For good reasons the book has, as far as I know, been steadily in print for 120 years now. There was a Disney movie, *King of the Grizzlies* (1970), based on it, though with a more upbeat ending than the book's.

Thirty-some years ago I began giving a talk to various audi-ences about the history of bears in Yellowstone National Park, the text of which eventually firmed up as the opening keynote at the

THE BIOGRAPHY OF A GRIZZLY
and
75 Drawings
by
ERNEST THOMPSON SETON

Author of
The Trail of the Sandhill Stag
Wild Animals I Have Known
Art Anatomy of Animals
Mammals of Manitoba
Birds of Manitoba

50. Ernest Thompson Seton was a skilled and gifted artist whose many books were generously illustrated with both light sketches and more detailed drawings. His title page for *The Biography of a Grizzly* (1900) is a good example. One can only guess the significance of the drawing of the oceanic volcano; perhaps it was meant to celebrate the long, complex, geological history of the Yellowstone landscape, which was shaped by many periods of volcanism and sedimentation.

park's third scientific conference, in 1995. It was duly published as "Yogi Lives: The Evolving Image of the Bears of Yellowstone." Looking back, I think I could more accurately have entitled it "The Expanding Image of the Bears of Yellowstone." The human idea of the bear has always been quite complex, but since Seton's time we have put the animal to work symbolizing things that were rarely thought of before the *Biography* was published; for one example, the idea of the bear as exemplifying the positive power and wonder of wilderness, not something you'd have heard much about before 1900, now dominates the animal's public image.

More often, however, we have just shifted our emphasis from one already existing part of the bear's image to another, and Seton's book provides a fine example of that shifting process, as the *Biography* heralded an overwhelming flood of children's books (including several placed in Yellowstone) that has never ceased. For many centuries before 1900, there must have been people who succumbed to the adorability of bear cubs, but it appears that Seton, in effect, launched the bear cub—and probably the adult bear—as a major literary project. The effects of this are untold and immeasurable, but it seems safe to say that at least some of the countless children who made their first acquaintance with bears through the tales of Wahb and his equally countless successors (see Pooh, in chapter 21 here, but let's also never forget Br'er bear, Baloo, Paddington, Teddy, Smokey et al., ad infinitum; and of course Jellystone's own Yogi) would carry their sympathies and affections for heroic bear-people along into adulthood.

The mass-produced early editions of the *Biography* are nonetheless lovely productions. That said, I still urge you to get the 2015 edition, entitled *Wahb: The Biography of a Grizzly*. This special edition retains all of Seton's hundreds of wonderful drawings along with the original text, but is greatly distinguished by its fine introduction by historian Jeremy Johnston and its equally erudite afterword by ecologist Charles (Chuck) Preston (also see my comments on this book, and a quote from Preston, back in chapter 3). The historical and modern worlds of Wahb are in the best possible hands when described by Jeremy and Chuck, who in this book have set a standard that I wish could be met in new annotated editions of several of the other early bear books on this list.

Seton often returned to the subject of bears in later works, writing about them in some of his more formal natural history works and writing another popular book-length fictional bear "biography," *Monarch the Big Bear of Tallac*.

But Seton's greatest accomplishment as a writer of bear natural history now seems almost forgotten. Over the course of a few years in the late 1920s, he produced his epic *Lives of Game Animals*, a monumental compendium that generously quoted many hundreds of sources about everything to do with dozens of species of wildlife, and illustrated it all with more than a thousand of his characteristic and helpful drawings. In antiquarian bookstores and catalogs today you will find this set of books listed as consisting of four "volumes," but there are actually eight large books, as each volume had two parts. The book we're concerned with here is volume 2, part 1, *Bears, Coons, Badgers, Skunks, and Weasels* (my copy is listed as published in Garden City by Doubleday, Doran and Company, 1929, but also lists 1909 and 1926 on the copyright page). The first 228 pages of this hefty, 367–page book are devoted to the bears of North America, and provide a fascinating and deeply anecdotal glimpse at the state of our understanding of everything to do with bears a century ago. It's also a superb sampler of the published sources of such information back then, when the best "outdoor" magazines still often featured the most reliable and even original nature studies. Among the many sources are quite a few that represent the earliest foundations of American bear science, produced by serious naturalists, and even zookeepers, who were able to provide lifelong observations of captive bears. Seton covered all the important topics about bears, including their complicated relationship with humans. He also treated his readers to many light-hearted little curiosities, such as "Can a Bear Count?" and "Playful Grizzlies—The Skunk." I can think of no other popularly published compendium of bear information that matched it until Gary Brown's 1993 thoroughly researched *Great Bear Almanac* expanded on Seton's effort and included all the world's bear species.

I have a lot of sympathy for what Seton was trying to do. Modern readers may think he was gullible in accepting some of the odder and more iffy reports he included, and he was regrettably dutiful in his loyalty to C. Hart Merriam's absurd splitting of the grizzly bear into dozens of spurious species (see Merriam later in this chapter). But look what he was up against back then. For most people, bears were either monsters or fairytale creatures, and for every account of bear life that Seton chose to include, he must have discarded reams of egregious misinformation, myths, and outright lies—and we're talking real industrial-grade bullshit here. If such obstacles weren't enough of a challenge to Seton's patience and good judgment, he had no way of knowing that Merriam, the nation's foremost bear scientist at the time, was leading not only Seton but every other serious bear student far off the taxonomic track by creating whole herds of new bear species.

Had a forward-looking publisher put this very text in its own book back then, not only would it have sold well, but we'd now rank Seton even higher than we do as a contributor to the growing public appreciation of bears and their world. For Seton, *Lives of Game Animals* amounted to a great vindication. Against the backdrop of criticism of his early work as anthropomorphic and unrealistic, the *Lives* won for him the American Museum of Natural History's supremely prestigious John Burroughs Medal for outstanding nature writing.

1900

Cincinnatus Heine "Joaquin" Miller

I am not sure what to do with, or even think about, Joaquin Miller's *True Bear Stories*, but it still felt right to include it. It is a book for children, addressed on its opening page to "My Bright Young Reader." According to Miller, it is based on his forty or so years of personal experiences with bears in many parts of the country, including the Pacific Coast states where he long lived but also Alaska and Louisiana. With this breadth of coverage and apparently personal acquaintance with grizzly, black, and polar bears, one would think that even a children's book would have sustained a greater reputation among readers of bear books. You'd also think that its references to scientific authority would entitle it to at least the level of credibility of other books from the period. And with laudatory "introductory notes" by no less prominent (if enduringly controversial) a scientific figure than David Starr Jordan, then president of Leland Stanford University, it sounds like the book should be a cornerstone of bear natural history rectitude.

So what's my problem with Miller's book? No doubt I am put on my guard by Ambrose Bierce's pronouncement that Miller was the "greatest liar this country ever produced. He cannot, or will not tell the truth." Miller did indeed have a sordid reputation in some circles. Any notable figure, especially one as clearly offbeat if not just annoying as Miller apparently was, will attract attacks by other offbeat notables (see Poe on Reid, presented earlier). I am also plainly given permission to disregard or at least not trust the book by California scientists Tracy Storer and Lloyd Tevis's assertion that *True Bear Stories* "was erroneous in both title and contents."

Or it could be that my problem with Miller just involves his "tone of voice," which even on my first reading of his book, long before I'd been warned about him, made me uneasy. On the other hand, many of these old bear books can be enjoyably and profitably read if the reader is alert for the errors and is even prepared to enjoy them. And all the better if the author was a famous liar; there's nothing like watching a master at work.

I suppose that if Miller hadn't so boldly titled his motley assortment of bear tales as something other than they turned out to be, I could have enjoyed, or just trusted, them more. Give his book a try and see if it strikes you any better.

1901

Charles Major

Charles Major, an Indiana attorney who practiced for many years in the late nineteenth and early twentieth centuries, wrote ten or so novels, more or less on the side, including the durable *The Bears of Blue River*, a novel for children set in 1820s Indiana. I have not seen the original edition of this, so I'm not absolutely certain of its publication information, but it has often been reprinted and is easily available in one edition or another, cloth, paper, and e-book. The book has obviously had considerable regional fame, and part of its legacy seems to be both a long-thriving but no-longer-held Bears of Blue River Festival in Shelbyville and a rock band named

51. The illustrations in Charles Major's durable and entertaining *The Bears of Blue River* (1901) present some of the most grizzlified black bears in popular bear literature. This individual bear features not only a somewhat caricatured grizzly bear conformation but also the ears of Spock and the nose of Pluto.

the Bears of Blue River. I assume that someone has written up the whole train of events and results that have followed from the original publication of the book, and perhaps an interested reader will track that down.

The book tells the story of the Balser Brent family, especially the son by that name and his many adventures in and around their frontier cabin. There's fishing, hunting for wolves, and of course many adventures with bears, which the book's illustrations quite ably portray as grizzly bears rather than the black bears they would have been. Perhaps the most intriguing episode in the novel (Major insisted it was based on a real incident) is the story of the "fire bear," an animal who, apparently having become coated by some naturally occurring phosphorescent substance in a cave, terror-ized the neighborhood on its nightly forays. Meaning no disrespect to the book, this episode involuntarily brings to mind that glorious scene in the 1983 film "Christine," when the "fiery Fury" blazes through the night. How exciting to imagine a bear doing the same thing with, much like Christine, no apparent harm to itself.

While I'm following this particular literary rabbit trail I might mention that this isn't the only bear book to feature a near-mythic fire bear. There's also Harold McCracken's (see chapter 22) novel *The Flaming Bear*, based on an Aleut oral tradition of a large bear that "glows like the moon on frosty winter nights" and is tracked down through great perils by the novel's young Aleut protagonist.

20

Early Experts

I might just as easily have called this chapter "early specialists" rather than early experts. By the close of the nineteenth century, the sport of hunting, the early stirrings of game management and wildlife biology, the creation of the first national parks, the emergence of the field of ecology, and—perhaps most important, in some ways—a rapidly growing publicly organized appreciation of a great variety of birds and mammals (for example, the Audubon movement, the Boone and Crockett Club, the Sierra Club) brought about an unprecedented appetite for reliable publications about wild places and their inhabitants. Most of the authors listed in this chapter had their start as part of one or more of those movements and grew up in that energetic time of change. Among those changes, the promise of Seton's early bear writings, such as *The Biography of a Grizzly*, profiled in the previous chapter, was fulfilled in a growing shelf of remarkably diverse bear books by hunters, naturalists, taxonomists, and other people passionate about everything to do with bears.

1908

Theodore Roosevelt

Theodore Roosevelt was both an outstanding adventure writer and a discerning and well-read naturalist. He seriously considered a career in wildlife study before turning to politics, and he never lost his keen fascination with the natural world. Like Lewis and Clark, he didn't intentionally write a bear book, but scattered among his many arti-

52. and 53. It is a happy irony that as distinguished a sportsman, conservationist, and naturalist as Theodore Roosevelt is now most closely associated in the public mind with the immense proliferation of cuddly bear toys, like these, which have long been mainstay souvenirs in many bear-country gift shops. Photos by author.

cles and books was a book's worth of the best, most thoughtful, and often most authoritative writing on bears to be had in his day. Long ago recognizing this, I put together just such a book, *American Bears: Selections from the Writings of Theodore Roosevelt*.

For the purposes of this list I have arbitrarily dated TR's contribution to the list as 1908 because that was the year the final chapter in "his" bear book was first published. It is a book of high wilderness adventure and insightful natural history. It is lacking, however, any mention of what may have been his most lasting contribution to the bear in American culture, because TR left it to others to chronicle how, based on certain awkward but memorable events during his 1902 black-bear hunt in Mississippi, he inspired the creation of the teddy bear.

It takes nothing away from Roosevelt's achievement as a writer on bears that, only a year after he finished writing the material that I gathered into *American Bears*, his probable if unrecognized preeminence as the nation's leading writer on bears was decisively undone by William Wright, whose landmark books are discussed next.

In the meantime, it is an amusing commentary on Roosevelt's continued strong appeal among both scholars and sportsmen that the first edition of *American Bears*, published by a fine university press in 1983, simultaneously appeared as an Outdoor Life Book Club dual main selection. Such uncommon breadth of academic and popular appeal would no doubt have pleased TR, just as it pleased me.

In her 1987 book *The Teddy Bear Men: Theodore Roosevelt and Clifford Berryman*, Linda Mullins provides a handsomely illustrated overview of the early proliferation of teddy bear imagery in America in Roosevelt's time. The public, of all ages, was clearly ready for a gentler, more personable portrayal of bears than had been most common in earlier times.

1909, 1910

William Henry Wright

William Wright is the only person who unquestionably deserves to make this list on the basis of either of two books, in his case

The Grizzly Bear: The Narrative of a Hunter-Naturalist (1909) and *Ben, the Black Bear* (1910). Both are milestones of bear writing, authoritative for their time, and characterized by a great admiration for bears, an ardent championing of the need for their conservation, and a lively manner of telling many still entertaining and provocative stories.

I talked my copy of *Ben, the Black Bear* out of the librarian in the little Vermont town where I lived in the late 1970s, for five bucks, mostly on the grounds that nobody had checked it out forever. I knew about *The Grizzly Bear*, but this was early enough in my research that I hadn't even heard of Wright's black-bear book until I came upon it in the library stacks while looking for something else. Like a few other of this list's authors, Wright tells the story of an orphaned bear cub he raised and learned from. This tale occupies the first half of the book. The second half is his fulsome description of the natural history of black bears generally.

It is one of the distinctions of *Ben* that it may be the first adult nonfiction bear book to have almost nothing to do with hunting (Ben came into Wright's possession after another hunter killed Ben's mother). In that respect, being a book about bears rather than a book about bear hunting, *Ben* anticipated others soon to come (see especially Mills, Underwood, and Skinner, later in this chapter).

In form and content, *The Grizzly Bear* set a general pattern for books that would be followed to one extent or another by such later classics as those by Harold McCracken and Andy Russell, as described in chapter 22. Wright began his saga of the grizzly bear with the earliest known sightings, then on to Lewis and Clark and their many successors, including Grizzly Adams, and on to the then prevailing scientific classification of the bears. This he followed with a wealth of personal experiences and a comprehensive review of the "character and habits" of the species. In both *Ben* and *The Grizzly Bear*, Wright devoted a few pages to reprinting the still-growing list of bears that the day's taxonomists, especially C. Hart Merriam (discussed later in this chapter), recognized as distinct species.

By the way, old Grizzly Adams has a fitting pride of place in the life and career of William Wright. Wright said that when he was a child in New Hampshire, his father would read to him from Hittell's biography of Adams, inspiring the boy to seek adventure. More than that, "in the early sixties," when Wright was six or so, his father took him to a Barnum circus in Nashua, where he saw a "huge grizzly, which was advertised as having been caught by this man Adams." This thrilling, tangible embodiment of great adventure solidified his dream to move to the West and live as Adams had. Wright even named Ben for Adams's pet grizzly bear Benjamin Franklin.

Wright was a keen and careful observer with a large and peril-ridden personal experience of both bear species. Early in my exploration of Yellowstone's bear-related literature, it was of particular interest to me that in his grizzly bear book he wrote at length about his stirring nighttime experiences near one of the park's dumps, photographing passing grizzly bears with early flash equipment. It still isn't hard to generate chills reading of that amazing (some would say amazingly foolhardy) adventure in pioneering wild-life photography. He also devoted much of a chapter in *Ben*, entitled "The Happy Hooligan," to the black bears he observed in Yellowstone.

1913

William D. Pickett

The book at issue here is *Hunting At High Altitudes* (1913), edited by George Bird Grinnell. I include this book for its first 294 pages, which are devoted to the life and hunting memoirs of William Pickett, with detailed commentary in notes by George Bird Grinnell. Alabama-born William D. Pickett, trained as an engineer and a veteran of both the war with Mexico and the Indian Wars in the American West, enlisted with the Confederacy and achieved the rank of colonel by the Civil War's end. He made his first hunting trip to the West in 1876, soon settling on the Greybull River east of Yellowstone National Park, where he earned notoriety as a great hunter of grizzly bears. First published in 1913 as one of a series of books sponsored by the Boone and Crockett Club (of which Pickett and Grinnell were both members; Grinnell and Theodore Roosevelt were the club's founders), his straightforward memoir of his many bear-hunting experiences was helpfully supported by Grinnell's expert historical and natural history commentary. Grinnell was one of the leading lights of the early conservation movement and intimately familiar with the region Pickett hunted.

Pickett is also of interest among readers of bear books because he is specifically named and portrayed by Seton, in a somewhat fictionalized version of himself, as the killer of Wahb's mother and siblings at the beginning of Seton's *Biography of a Grizzly*. Seton did not necessarily do this as a compliment of any sort to Pickett, but I sometimes suspect that Pickett, a dedicated killer of bears, either wouldn't have minded or would even have enjoyed this literary notoriety.

1918

Clinton Hart Merriam

Here we come to an oddly pivotal landmark in the literature of the grizzly bear. C. Hart Merriam, perhaps the nation's leading "splitter" of his day—the nickname was given to scientists inclined to break familiar species down into more and more separate species or subspecies—reached his most dazzling if not dizzying heights in that respect with the publication in 1918 of his *Review of the grizzly and big brown bears of North America (genus Ursus) with description of a new genus, Vetularctos*. At no cost, you can now download this remarkable document, which threw the mother of all monkey wrenches into the study of North American grizzly bear taxonomy for nearly half a century.

Merriam, often called the father of mammalogy, was a giant figure in wildlife science during his long and extremely productive career, which ran from about 1870 to well into the 1900s. He headed the U.S. Bureau of Biological Survey for twenty-five years, was influential in the formalization of federal government science, voraciously gathered priceless scientific data of various kinds from many parts of the country, and published hugely in various disciplines from ornithology to ethnology. I've long enjoyed my

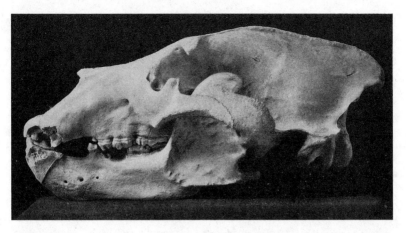

54. Clinton Hart Merriam's enormous collection of precisely calipered bear skulls formed the basis for his influential but now wholly disregarded monograph, *Review of the Grizzly and Big Brown Bears of North America* (1918), in which this photograph appeared.

facsimile edition of his classic monograph *The Mammals of the Adirondack Region* (1884). And he was a mighty presence on the bear science scene.

But as I said, he had a thing about the defining of species, and nowhere is it more clearly and—retroactively at least—embarrassingly displayed than in his wondrous and awful 1918 monograph of grizzly and brown bears. Basing his species distinctions primarily on cranial and dental measurements, Merriam identified no less than eighty-six distinct species of grizzly and brown bear, and very nearly apologized that "there are very many gaps in the series" even at that.

It's important to keep Merriam in context though; apparently quite a few people agreed with him. Others, perhaps most notably his friend Theodore Roosevelt, didn't. But we should remember that to many people, including some of the most authoritative writers in this bear book list, Merriam was the premier scientific authority on bears and not to be argued with.

Indeed, according to scientists Tracy Storer and Lloyd Tevis, writing in the mid-1950s, "because of Dr. Merriam's long preoccupation with the bears, other mammalogists did little with them."

Reading that explained a lot to me as I puzzled over what seemed to me a disproportionate lack of scientific interest in bears in the early 1900s. To make matters worse, as Merriam was known to be working on a book about bears, it is possible that knowledge of this impending volume further discouraged similar projects by other scientists and perhaps even by popular writers.

Merriam's monograph represented the historic peak of the splitting fashion in bear science. Though, as we will see, respectful references to his list of species continued to pop up in other people's publications well into the 1950s, by the 1920s the excesses of his classifications were being questioned and steadily simplified and were eventually swept entirely away. In 1945 the prominent paleontologist George Gaylord Simpson largely dismissed Merriam's whole system as mistaking minor variations between individual bears as proof of new species, pointing out that "in such a system twin bear cubs could be of different species."

In 1953 mammalogist Robert Rausch, observing that "the specific status of North American grizzly bears is one of the most complex problems in mammalian taxonomy," laid the "difficulty" squarely on Merriam's doorstep. Based on his work with arctic bears, Rausch proposed that the brown and grizzly bears of North America, for all their diversity, were all the same species with a few probable subspecies. Scientifically at least, that was pretty much the end of Merriam's classification. Since then, three generations and still going, it's been about coming to terms with a small number of possible species or subspecies designations, and if you see a grizzly bear anywhere in North America, except on a few of the islands of coastal Alaska, it's all the same bear.

But Merriam's monograph is still worth a browse. Wrong-headed as it turned out to be, its carefully calipered skulls document a scientific travelogue of bear landscapes all the way from Mexico to the Far North. True, the numbingly technical descriptions of the tiniest features of individual skulls are unreadable in a normal state of mind, but that's not what Merriam's monograph is good for anyway. It's just an amazing and somehow humbling thing to leaf through and wonder at now and then. I still do. Give it a try; after all, it's free.

1919

Enos Abijah Mills

As with William Wright's books, Mills's *The Grizzly, Our Greatest Wild Animal* (1919) has long been recognized as an early milestone in the making of bear books. My copy of *The Grizzly* still has the receipt from a little mail-order, used-book store in Ontario, indicating that in 1978 I was willing to spend a wildly extravagant twenty dollars for it. I know I've mentioned making these purchases-that-felt-like-major-investments before, but it's hard to overstate, especially for today's younger readers, that back in those days of infrequently delivered and long-studied mimeographed catalogs from remote, out-of-print book dealers, the finding, ordering, and finally receiving in the mail of such a book could be an event of almost holiday proportions.

In 1889, when he was about nineteen, Mills happened to meet the great California naturalist and conservationist John Muir, an encounter that is said to have inspired his life's direction. Among Mills's distinctions, he was so forceful a leader in the campaign that led to the creation of Rocky Mountain National Park that he is often referred to as the father of that great wilderness park.

A bear biologist friend, a scientist of unquestioned expertise, found some of Mills's stories so implausible that he couldn't even finish reading the book. No doubt when I first read it I was under the optimistic influence of wanting to believe that my sizeable financial commitment in it was not a mistake, but even today I have a lot of sympathy for Mills and his stories. Despite the criticisms I offer of several of the books on this list, I continue to believe that if you're going to explore these profoundly sincere attempts to portray American bears—portrayals written mostly by people whose opinions and certainties were largely based on their own, often extensive and occasionally fearful personal experiences—you should be prepared to give them a break. At best you're looking for consensus rather than unanimous agreement among them, and for trends in their viewpoints from generation to generation. On those terms, Mills is great reading.

And, checking in on Merriam's taxonomy, Mills dutifully devoted eleven pages near the back of his book to a thorough quoting of Merriam's sprawling list of imagined North American grizzly and brown bear species, discussed immediately above. He would not be the last to do so.

1921

Henry Wharton Shoemaker

Early in the 1900s, prominent newspaperman-historian-folklorist Henry Shoemaker was an energetic collector of information on many aspects of early Pennsylvania history. He published numerous small books on various subjects, including several on wildlife, and this is his gathering of bear stories from various informants and local newspapers. There's a lot to be said for period books like this, which are about as close as we can now come to the undiluted realities of what any given set of locals thought, said, and did about bears in their part of the country in their day.

Shoemaker's 1921 book *The Black Bear of Pennsylvania*, a compilation of writings by various people, was an early entry in a still-growing subset of bear books—those about a specific geographic area, most often an individual state or maybe a national park. What with the wealth of raw informational material at hand, especially in the form of anecdotal accounts from journals, interviews, newspapers and other periodicals, but more and more frequently in competent scientific research findings, there's a lot to be said for a writer narrowing down his or her focus this way. The subject becomes manageable, and the variabilities inherent in, say, a bear population's ecology, also may become a tad less daunting. If your region, state, or neighborhood still lacks such a book, you might want to think about writing it.

1921

William Lyman Underwood

William Lyman Underwood's 1921 *Wild Brother: Strangest of True Stories from the North Woods* is a remarkable story, a strikingly different twist on the common we-adopted-a-bear-cub story. In February 1903 Boston businessman and photographer William Lyman Underwood encountered a rural Maine family that had adopted an orphaned black bear cub. The woman was nursing the cub along with her own infant, a daughter fittingly named Ursula. His book contains many photographs of little "Bruno," the most famous and no doubt most scandalous—the ancient and widespread practice of interspecies nursing still being disturbing to many people—being a photo of the human mother nursing her own infant and Bruno at the same time. It is a lovely and touching picture.

Underwood seems to have handled this obviously sensational story with tact and respect. He protected the family's privacy by giving them a fictitious name and providing only vague descriptions of where all this was happening. As Bruno became larger and more difficult for the family to manage, Underwood took the young bear home to raise; his eventful experiences in doing so make up about two-thirds of the book. Before Bruno was three he became unruly and dangerous enough that Underwood regretfully put him in a zoo, where he lived until his death at age fourteen.

1925

Milton Philo Skinner

Milton Skinner's 1925 *Bears in the Yellowstone* is another notable early bear book with a limited (well, 2.2 million acres, anyway) geographical focus. I still remember my excitement, at least forty-five years ago, upon finding this book on the shelf of a long-gone but still-lamented used-book shop just off West Main Street in Bozeman. Even in the early 1970s it was the only adult book ever published about the bears I was just then trying to explain to park visitors, and though by the time I bought it in the early 1970s real scientists had been hard at work studying Yellowstone's bears for more than a decade, there was still nothing else like Skinner's book available for the general reader, though there soon would be several.

Longtime Yellowstone-area naturalist Milton Skinner's *Bears in the Yellowstone* was the first extended attempt at an observation-based natural history of both park bear species. When I first came

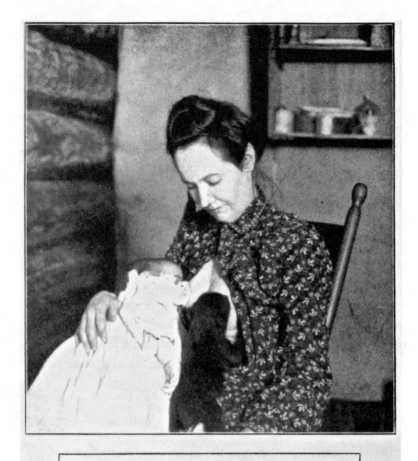

Mr Underwood took this picture of Ursula and Bruno and me with my consent and I am glad to have him use it in this book.
                    Bruno's Foster Mother

55. Out of respect for the family's privacy, William Lyman Underwood did not disclose the name or exact location (in backwoods Maine) of the woman who nursed and raised an orphan black bear cub along with her infant daughter. Photo from Underwood's *Wild Brother* (1921).

upon Skinner's writings I was skeptical, and I'm still sure that some of his forays into the history of Yellowstone wildlife were sadly erroneous. But when I look through this book I'm impressed by some of his helpful and even quantitative inquiries into bear behavior and physical features. He was a functioning field naturalist who paid attention to details in a way only possible for a person who'd spent years at it. For one telling example, here is Skinner on the color of Yellowstone black bears:

> In ten years I have seen 228 black bears to 241 of lighter shade. Where I have been able to distinguish the sex, the larger number of females have been brown, and the males black; but this may be only a coincidence and not true of the whole bear population. There is no judging the color of the offspring by that of the parents, for the cubs may be of three or four colors and some or all may differ from the parents. But whatever color a black bear may be, it is the same color throughout except possibly on the nose and breast.

For a young and information-starved Yellowstone ranger like me, a concentrated blast of firsthand observations like these, even if they were nearly half a century old, was still pure gold. Other observers since then have confirmed his statements more broadly; while almost all eastern black bears are black, half or so of inland western ones are lighter colors. Thanks, Milt, and you would probably be interested but maybe not surprised to hear that if you continue west from Yellowstone, once you get to the heavily forested Pacific Coast, most of the black bears are, with a few notable exceptions, again black.

21

Myths, Legends, and a Bear of Very Little Brain

T
he broadening of subject matter in bear books during the past century is cause for great delight among readers. The basic forms—hunting adventure, natural history, scientific study, fictional portrayals—were mostly in place by the time of Skinner's book on Yellowstone bears, but there seems to have been no end of topical side trips to make in our exploration of the bear's world and in all the little corners it inhabited in our imaginations. As long as there are bears and people to encounter them, I'm sure that exploration will continue.

1926

Alan Alexander Milne

Fumbling, honey-obsessed little Winnie-the-Pooh has ranked among the world's most famous and beloved bears for upwards of a century now. A. A. Milne's book *Winnie-the-Pooh* and its sequel *The House at Pooh Corner* have been hugely popular, as have a nearly steady stream of music, films, and authorized sequels. If you are a more-than-casual Pooh enthusiast, you should be alerted to the existence, in other of Milne's publications, of a few more vagrant stories about Pooh or Pooh-like characters.

I especially enjoy that Pooh was, in a way, twice fictional. Not only was he a character in a work of fiction, he was not a "real" bear at all; he was a sewn-up child's toy in the best teddy bear manner. This makes him all the more interesting a literary cre-

56. In 1914, in White River, Ontario, a young Canadian lieutenant, Harry Colebourn, bought a black bear cub, named her Winnie (in honor of his hometown of Winnipeg), and more or less smuggled her to England as his regiment's mascot. Colebourn, just then on his way to the war in Europe, gave her to the London Zoo, where she lived for many years and inspired young Christopher Milne to name his teddy bear for her, which likewise inspired Christopher's father, A. A. Milne, who wrote the immortal Winnie-the-Pooh stories. White River has a lovely park and memorial, seen here, honoring their place in this literary saga. Photo by author.

ation. Being by his own admission "a Bear of Very Little Brain," Pooh may at first glance seem to have little to offer us beyond his own enduring sweetness (which, by the way, I am certain is quite enough if that's just the sort of character you happen to be in the mood for). But literary scholars have—and rightly, I think—made much of him and his equally fictional companions. And even if said scholars may sometimes strain the subject at hand in their critical dissections (see Faulkner in this chapter), there should be no doubt that Pooh's brain is plenty big enough to think thoughts of respectable consequence. As well, Pooh provides us a telling contrast with the likes of Wahb, thus suggesting the vast literary opportunities that bears, by their very nature and complications of personality, offer us.

In 1978, as I was working on the first edition of *The Bears of Yellowstone*, I realized that the section of my book about bear management needed help from Pooh. Specifically, I wanted to open my discussion of the long, painful controversy over divorcing Yellowstone bears from human garbage with the lines from the enchanting Kenny Loggins song, "House at Pooh Corner," that describe sending Pooh to ask the Owl how to "loosen a jar" from a bear's nose. Those lines couldn't have been a more perfect metaphor for the search for the wisdom and practical tool kit needed to unhook Yellowstone's bears from campground discards and hotel leftovers. But at the time, the song's publisher, apparently just then involved in some messy legal dispute over the rights to that very song, refused me permission.

1926

Alfred Irving Hallowell

Anthropologist-archeologist Alfred Irving Hallowell's "Bear Ceremonialism in the Northern Hemisphere" appeared as an article in the January–March 1926 edition of the journal *American Anthropologist*. But as its 175 pages of profusely documented text occupied almost that entire number of the journal, I'm comfortable enough with its essential "bookness" to include it here. Indeed, it's too important to leave out.

For a long time I had to make do with a photocopy of this great milestone of bear literature, though now it's also easily available as a download. I like to think that eventually one of the many print-on-demand outfits that have brought many thousands of obscure titles back into paper existence will eventually come upon Hallowell's monograph and make it available as a "real" book. Maybe they already have and I've just missed it.

Hallowell took a broad, long view of the human relationship with bears, exploring how circumpolar "primitive peoples" (not a term we're happy with any more, but like all the authors on this list, Hallowell was a person of his time) perceived, hunted, named, artistically celebrated, spoke with, put to practical use, and most especially ceremonialized whichever species of bear or bears shared their realms. Concerning bear ceremonialism, Hallowell brought together a fascinating and at times startling body of information that even today we may read to our great advantage and stimulation.

Here again I can't help breaking my rule about mentioning post–1967 books to recommend to you two splendid books that add substantially to the scholarly tradition that Hallowell was pioneering: Paul Shepard and Barry Sanders's *The Sacred Paw: The Bear in Nature, Myth, and Literature* and David Rockwell's *Giving Voice to Bear: North American Indian Myths, Rituals, and Images of the Bear*. As I write this, I also look forward to the publication of what sounds like an extremely valuable new title, editors Heather A. Lapham and Gregory A. Waselkov's *Bears: Archeological and Ethnohistorical Perspectives in Native Eastern North America*.

1929

Theodore Roosevelt Jr. and Kermit Roosevelt

It wasn't until 1869 that the giant panda—typically just called the panda—was first seen by a westerner, and even that was just a hide rather than a living animal. The honor of that first "sighting" went to Père Armand David, a missionary and sometime collector of specimens. In *The Giant Pandas of Wolong*, by George B. Schaller, Hu Jinchu, Pen Wensi, and Zhu Jing (1985), we are told that "Pere David's desire 'to kill this carnivore' was also to become the goal of all Western hunters and museum collectors who visited the panda's range in the 70 years following the scientific discovery." The Roosevelts were the first westerners to successfully shoot a panda and bring its hide home, and their book *Trailing the Giant Panda* tells of their struggles and adventures in doing so.

These sons of the late president, both prominent citizens in their own rights and veterans of both world wars (Theodore was a Medal of Honor winner in World War II), were lifelong sportsmen and conservationists who led two expeditions to Asia to collect museum specimens. Kermit was especially familiar with extended international expeditions, having accompanied his father on TR's famously long safari in Africa (1909–10) and on the far more hazardous exploration of Brazil's River of Doubt (1913–14), whose hardships nearly killed both father and son.

Trailing the Giant Panda tells the story of the brothers' second Asian expedition, the Kelley–Roosevelt–Field Museum Expedition of 1929, a full-fledged research party including a number of scientific specialists. The book follows the brothers on that portion of the trip they took specifically to collect a giant panda and a few other rarely seen large mammals. Being their father's sons, they paid what attention they could to the natural history of the species of large mammals they sought, their observations resulting in natural history findings both in the text and in an appendix entitled "Zoographical Notes on the Sino Tibetan Borderland."

It was a long trip, more than four months of often difficult hiking, horse-, or mule-back travel with extended portions of the route above ten thousand feet—and passes at or more than fifteen thousand feet—through remarkably varying weather including long stretches in deep snow. Their experiences on previous expeditions taught them the wisdom of bringing previously produced pictures of the species they sought, which they showed to anyone likely to know where to find such animals. They were surprised that even within a day's travel of panda habitat, most of the local hunters and town bureaucrats they met along the way had never seen or even heard of the secretive panda, whose near invisibility has been a challenge for many researchers since then. Besides the specimen they eventually shot, they did manage to purchase the hides of two other pandas.

Certainly they were men of their times, keen adventurers who spent their entire lives in the long shadow of their more famous sportsman-naturalist-president father. And just as certainly their expedition's goals were scientific and greatly to the advantage of their museum sponsor and the vast public who would benefit from that museum's collections. But reading their account of the day they finally located and shot a rare, shy, slow-moving animal that had spent its whole life up to that minute quietly munching bamboo stems, I find myself, as Schaller found himself when he first read their book, "reluctant to applaud their success."

1930

John Michael Holzworth

John Holzworth's 1930 *The Wild Grizzlies of Alaska* has been a great favorite of mine since I found it during my early bear reading (another twenty-dollar extravagance, and a bargain at that, considering even just its size and classy production). From its foreword by the famous zoologist-conservationist William T. Hornaday, through its vivid and photographically bedecked accounts of Holzworth's experiences with the giant brown bears of Alaska, to its literary and natural history of grizzly and brown bears generally, *The Wild Grizzlies of Alaska* epitomizes a passionate and deeply sympathetic portrayal of the animals the author dearly loved.

Roughly half the book is devoted to a series of trips Holzworth made to Alaska in the late 1920s, mostly to Admiralty Island, around which he traveled in company with Allen E. Hasselborg, "philosopher and friend," as well as being yet another on our list of notable bear-hunters-turned-naturalists. On these trips Holzworth was exposed to many misconceptions and "myths" about bears that he outlined later in the book. The book is further distinguished by more than one hundred photographs, including some single pages on which he reproduced three strips of movie film showing (all too small, but it was a good idea anyway), in a sequence of more than twenty successive frames, the behavior of one of the bears.

Among the hidden literary treats in the book is an entire article, "The Last Stand of the Bear," by Harry McGuire, longtime editor of *Outdoor Life* and a now largely forgotten advocate for bear conservation. But then, from a certain perspective, the whole book is one big treat. And the photos, despite their age and the limitations of the technology that put them in the book, are wonderful.

Holzworth wrote another sizeable bear book, *The Twin Grizzlies of Admiralty Island* (1932), a fictionalized account of the lives of a pair of bear cubs whose story he learned from Hasselborg, who originally captured them in about 1912. It is illustrated with fifteen of Holzworth's Admiralty Island photographs. You should also know that Hasselborg's life and experiences are the subject of a thorough biography by John R. Howe, *Bear Man of Admiralty Island: A Biography of Allen E. Hasselborg.*

1938

Ruth Harkness

Ruth Harkness was an American socialite-turned-adventurer whose husband, Bill, attempted to find a panda in China but died of cancer in Shanghai in 1936. Taking on her husband's goal, she made a series of trips to China. On her first trip in late 1936, working with local experts as must all such expeditions, she became the first person to bring a live panda cub back to the United States, where it resided for a time at Chicago's Brookfield Zoo. On a second trip in 1937 she succeeded in returning with another panda cub. She told of her story in *The Lady and the Panda: An Adventure* and *The Baby Giant Panda.* Her story has been told more recently by Vicki Croke, *The Lady and the Panda: The True Adventures of the First American Explorer to Bring Back China's Most Exotic Animal* (2005).

Harkness's books unknowingly described the beginning of what remains today a complicated and controversial enterprise—the obtaining from China of pandas for exhibition by many of the world's foremost zoos. From the arrival of Harkness's first captive panda, named Su-Lin, at the Brookfield Zoo in 1936, panda exhibition has grown into a costly and profitable business, with zoos paying in the neighborhood of a million dollars a year to "rent" a panda, whose transfer from China to a foreign zoo may coincide with international trade favors between China and the host nation.

Tightly managing both their wild and captive panda populations, China has maintained a monopoly on panda ownership (any cubs born to rent-a-panda couples while they are abroad contractually remain Chinese property). Whatever the various contestants in the conservation-related controversies may say about this situation, it is unquestionably a fascinating topic in the modern study of wildlife economics and yet one more colorful twist in the history of bears and people.

By the way, in addition to his coauthorship of the pioneering scientific book on pandas mentioned earlier (see also the Roosevelts earlier in this chapter), I should mention that George Schaller's popularly written memoir of that research, *The Last Panda*, is absorbing reading.

But there are many more panda books now, to the point that when I browse the book shops and websites for panda-related titles, I wonder if there aren't more books than there are wild pandas.

1942

William Faulkner

Various versions of William Faulkner's story "The Bear" were published in periodicals, as a stand-alone novelette, and as a chapter in anthologies in different forms before or after its most famous appearance in the novel-like collection of stories entitled *Go Down, Moses*. Its eventual additional solo publication as an independent work gives me plenty of room to include it in a list of bear books, though I would feel compelled to include it even had it never appeared between covers of its own. And I still think it best to read the story in the context of a complete reading of *Go Down, Moses*.

I'm leery of simplistic rankings, but it's worth explaining that, just as many well-read sportsmen regard Ernest Hemingway's "Big Two-Hearted River" as the best American fishing story, so do they regard "The Bear" as the best American hunting story. Faulkner being Faulkner, and Faulkner scholarship being Faulkner scholarship, the actual hunting tale, and especially the bear "character," have been routinely subsumed beneath a welter of greater symbolisms, themes, and critical interpretations. Critical vivisection without end is just what we literary types do.

That said, during my heaviest bear-reading days, when I enthusiastically read the scholarly compendium *Bear, Man, and God: Eight Approaches to William Faulkner's "The Bear,"* edited by Francis Utley, Lynn Bloom, and Arthur Kinney, I was both gratified at their understanding of so much of the historic bear-hunting literature and stumped by the way this crew of excellent scholars mostly ignored the bear itself in preference to Faulkner studies' mainstream academic topics of southern history, heroism, race, moral order, and so on. I haven't in the least kept up on Faulkner scholarship since then, but I hope that someone has done a better job of celebrating what a fantastic job Faulkner did in portraying an animal that at his hands manages to be both an ecological reality and a mythic monster, and, at least for those of us who like bears, is easily one of the most memorable characters in the book.

1943

Montague Stevens

Rather like my reaction to Joaquin Miller's book, but not as extreme, I have never warmed to Montague Stevens's *Meet Mr. Grizzly: A Saga on the Passing of the Grizzly Bear,* but several commentators whose opinions I admire and trust think highly of it, so I am happy to recommend it. Stevens's affection for bears is evident throughout, and his knowledge and experience of them was obviously extensive.

More than most other books on the list, this is almost purely a hunting book, but it is a hunting book in an inclusive and informative way. If, for example, you love stories of dogs, especially hunting dogs of various sorts, you may enjoy his lively and affectionate stories of developing an effective pack of bear-hunting dogs.

As hunters go, Stevens was astonishing. English, a Cambridge graduate, and reasonably well off, he settled in New Mexico in the early 1880s. He lost his left arm in a hunting accident in 1888, but the next year began to hunt grizzly bears, following his dogs on many wild and hairy horseback outings, somehow managing to handle a horse, a rifle, and eventually a seriously perturbed bear with only one arm. That alone makes his book enormously appealing to readers of hunting adventures.

Apparently Stevens's active years as grizzly bear hunter ended after only a decade or so, following which he said he "became a zealous convert to their preservation, to prevent so noble an animal becoming extinct." Not that it made any noticeable difference, as the grizzly bears of the Southwest were nearly gone by the time his book came out, but at least he got around to the right idea eventually.

If the history of the bears of that beautiful and ecologically diverse region interests you, I must recommend David Brown's outstanding *The Grizzly in the Southwest: Documentary of an Extinction*, which does for those long-lamented bears what Storer and Tevis's *California Grizzly* (see chapter 22) did for the Golden State's bears.

22

A Modern Sensibility

Recognizing that the chronological divisions that I have introduced into the history of bear books are somewhat artificial, I still think a case can be made that by the middle of the last century bear literature had "arrived" in something very like a modern form (whether it was approaching some *post-modern* form would require an essay I wouldn't enjoy writing, almost as much as you wouldn't enjoy reading it). A good part of my reasoning here is based on the extent to which some of the books in this chapter are backward looking—heavily focused as much on what bears have *been* as on what they are now—and the disheartening extent to which those same books must warn us of the often gloomy future facing many bear populations.

For balance, I've included some exceptions here; Beatty's little book on the bears of Yosemite is a miniature of what Skinner did for the bears of Yellowstone a generation earlier, and Spencer's monograph is a model of midcentury wildlife management narrative. But in most of the following titles there is a heightened alarm, either stated or implied, about what we're going to make of the bears next.

1946

Matthew Edward Beatty

I happily strain most definitions of a real book to include here Matthew Beatty's little *Bears of Yosemite*, which first appeared as an extended article in *Yosemite Nature Notes* vol. 22, no. 1 (January

1943): 1–17. In 1946 it was reprinted as a seventeen-page booklet by the Yosemite Natural History Association. Beatty was associate park naturalist in Yosemite for many years in the 1930s and 1940s, but by the time the booklet appeared he had transferred to Glacier National Park as that park's chief naturalist where, I am disappointed to report, he did *not* write a similar little book about the bears of Glacier.

From the 1920s to the 1960s many American national parks regularly published their own "nature notes" several times a year. These were written by each park's naturalist staff, often with additional contributions from other park residents. Most seem to have been mimeographed. They were distributed to park employees and to some number of other interested parties, and they remain a deep source of anecdotal material about park history, wildlife, other natural and cultural features, and management issues. In the nature notes from several of the larger parks, bears were routinely a featured topic, as any of those parks that were inhabited by bears were experiencing the same perpetual turmoil in attempting to manage the bears and visitors so that neither did too much harm to the other. My historical anthology *Yellowstone Bear Tales: Adventures, Mishaps, and Discoveries among the World's Most Famous Bears* would have been a lot thinner and less fun without so many tales drawn from *Yellowstone Nature Notes*.

Beatty started with a brief account of the by-then extinct California grizzly bear. There followed a competent review of Yosemite black bear natural history and a summary of the park's bear-management policies and plans. The narrative was illuminated throughout by stories of individual bears and illustrated with black-and-white photographs. It is a charming period piece and yet another testament to the public's long fascination with and affection for park bears.

1955

Tracy Irwin Storer and Lloyd Pacheco Tevis Jr.

In their book *California Grizzly*, scientists Storer and Tevis performed a magnificent public service by sifting through mountainous quantities of historical material to document the life and ways of these wonderful animals in that once-paradisiacal realm. Exhaustively documented, it is yet hospitable in tone and consistently entertaining.

Having reconstructed the life and natural world of the historic California grizzly bear to the furthest extent possible, Storer and Tevis continued with a delightfully exhaustive review of the bear in the human cultures of old California, tracking its meanings and participation in the various native and European American societies that have taken turns dominating the human aspects of the California landscape. Grizzly Adams, as still the most popular human story in this saga, gets a whole, well-researched, and carefully thought-out chapter to himself. The ongoing and evolving symbolism of the California grizzly bear up to the time of the book's publication is likewise considered. They even take considerable pains to consider skeptically the species issues raised by Merriam, reviewing the arguments of his various later critics.

In my first years as a historian of wildlife and human-wildlife interactions, I quickly recognized this book as a model of how effectively and rewardingly such studies can be conducted. For all its formidable scholarly rectitude, it is still the sort of book one might take down from the shelf for some rewarding browsing on a long winter evening. And, as mentioned earlier in the discussion of Theodore Hittell's book about Grizzly Adams, the Storer-Tevis book now enjoys an outstanding companion volume, Susan Snyder's *Bear in Mind: The California Grizzly*.

1955

Harold McCracken

Harold McCracken's *The Beast That Walks Like Man: The Lore, Legend and History of the Grizzly Bear* was a generous gathering of the lore and history of the grizzly bear. I have already admitted my approval of it by writing an extended introductory essay for a handsome new edition, with the subtitle changed to "The Story of the Grizzly Bear," and published in 2003 by Roberts Rinehart.

57. Grizzly country: Yoho National Park in the Canadian Rockies. Photo by author.

Maybe it's only because of my enthusiasm for the bear and the historical world it has tried to inhabit that I don't mind reading, in McCracken's book, yet another retelling of the adventures of Lewis and Clark, Grizzly Adams, and various other early adventurers who encountered the grizzly bear. It helps that McCracken, being a prominent and honored student of western history and culture, gave us so much more of that engaging material than did most of his predecessors who covered the same ground—and that he could place those very predecessors in the same ongoing saga. Besides, McCracken added substantially to the literature of personal experience with bears, based mostly on his years among them in Alaska.

Among the odd distinctions of McCracken's book is that despite some three decades of ongoing scientific dismantling of Merriam's 1918 list of eighty-six grizzly bear species, McCracken respectfully reprinted the whole list in an appendix. I'm not sure whether he did that out of ignorance of the subsequent science, because he actually preferred Merriam's approach to the North American bears, or because he regarded such rarified science simply as beyond his range of authority. But I believe this was the last significant appearance in a popular book of Merriam's list before his fading reputation could no longer credibly buttress it in the face of less extravagant views.

Like so many of the earlier writers in this list, McCracken came to believe in the importance of conserving bear populations. Having already described his views on that matter as well as I could in my introduction to the new edition of his book, I will quote myself here:

> We are hard-pressed to find individuals who bring more of the necessary qualities for bear conservationists—who will serve us as better exemplars of the kinds of friends the bear will need—than Harold McCracken. We are all products of our times, and no doubt future bear protectors will need and embrace new ideas and new sensibilities that have eluded us so far, just as we have abandoned some of the things that McCracken knew to be true. But it's a sure thing that it will be in an all-encompassing breadth of awareness—of everything from the bear as art, as brother, as icon, and as quarry to the bear as scientific marvel and barometer of wilderness health—that we will best serve the species in the future. Harold McCracken proved that.

A regular writer of books for young people, McCracken produced at least three other bear books: *Alaska Bear Trails*, *The Biggest Bear on Earth*, and the previously mentioned *The Flaming Bear*.

1961

Howard E. Spencer Jr.

As I've already mentioned (see Shoemaker, above), I appreciate books that are confined to some specific and comparatively contained region. Spencer's *The Black Bear and Its Status in Maine* is among the first such science-based management studies of a state's bear population. I want to give it attention here as more or less representative of several similar studies made in other states in the 1960s and 1970s.

At fifty-five pages it is more a report or monograph than a book but as I've already suggested we're not into this to quibble over bibliographical terminology. It's a separate work with its own (rather pretty) cover.

Spencer started with a concise summary of black bear natural history in Maine, including calculations of the state's bear population—a heroic exercise that I have always found interesting wherever it is undertaken, as the author had to quantify his way through so many knowns, unknowns, and variables. Spencer's calculations do, in fact, demonstrate just how far such estimates had come from the seat-of-the-pants guesswork earlier in the century.

From this reasonably firm footing, Spencer moved along to the more pressing and pragmatic issues facing bear managers. Central among these were (and are) bear "depredations," most involving livestock, pets, and crops but also property damage when bears broke into buildings or made the most of apiaries (see Pooh, above). Naturally, bear hunting and trapping were important features of the bear's socioeconomic value. In Maine, at the time, bears were still being hunted for a bounty, and there was a legal market for bear meat, which successful bear trappers could sell publicly. Spencer's assertion that the "recreational value of the bear in Maine was impossible to assess in dollars and cents" anticipated later generations of wildlife economists, who would make credible efforts to produce just such assessments, but he was certain that even though he couldn't put an exact price tag on the bear's "recreational and economic value," he was at least sure that its potential value was a good bit higher than its realized value.

I should probably mention another similar but more extensive early state report—Albert Erickson, John Nellor, and George Petrides, *The Black Bear in Michigan* (Ann Arbor: Michigan State University Agricultural Experiment Station, Research Bulletin 4, 1964), that is of at least equal interest. Erickson was, by the way, one of the modern pioneers of black bear research and went on to very productive studies of the bears of Alaska.

1966

Bessie Haynes and Edgar Haynes

Bessie and Edgar Haynes's *The Grizzly Bear: Portraits from Life* is, as far as I know, still the best, most generous, and diverse sam-

58. Black bear country: the Rangeley Lake region in western Maine. Photo by author.

pling of North American bear literature under one cover, though there are now a few others that also do a good job and, being more recent, may contain some fresher material. Haynes and Haynes had a good eye for many of the most interesting, exciting, and colorful of writings by a broad assortment of mountain men, explorers, hunters, naturalists, and tourists.

This is as good a place as any to point out and even complain about the authorship imbalances that are inherent in a book list of this sort, and from these dates. The Haynes and Haynes book, like most other anthologies of bear stories (including two of my own), does not include meaningful material from Native American traditions. Nor do women have much to say; following the editors' coauthored introduction, the first female writer whose work is included in this book appears in chapter 38, when the book is three-quarters finished. It was only after my 1967 deadline for this list that women writers, speaking as journalists, scientists, wildlife managers, conservationists, and from other perspectives, became prominent and highly respected contributors to nonfiction bear literature.

1967

Andy Russell

I've already explained my devotion to Andy Russell's *Grizzly Country* (in chapters 2 and 18). By good luck it was one of the first bear books I found and was for its time truly essential. It was a nearly instant classic not only for its sweeping account of the grizzly and brown bears of North America but for the spirited immediacy of its author's many firsthand adventures in bear country as rancher, hunter, guide, naturalist, and filmmaker. I suppose my reading preferences are as subjective and whimsical as the next person's, but for whatever set of reasons *Grizzly Country* has always suited me just right. I still enjoy rereading it every few years, certainly more often than any other bear book published before or since.

I have also become such an admirer of *Grizzly Country* because it was a handsome product of the venerable and extraordinarily distinguished Alfred A. Knopf–Borzoi Books publishing enterprise. Mention that name to most *normal* serious readers and they'll more likely think of the long list of Nobel and Pulitzer Prize winners published by Knopf. But for people like me (and, I suspect, you) it will bring to mind great and elegantly published books on nature and outdoor sport by not only Russell but also George Schaller, Jack O'Connor, Sigurd Olsen, and others.

Besides *Grizzly Country*, Russell scattered writings on bears throughout several other of his excellent books. He also edited a generous anthology of bear stories by many writers past and present, *Great Bear Adventures: True Tales from the Wild*. His introduction to that book is itself a good contribution to bear reading; among other things it includes a candidly genial comment about his years spent filming grizzly bears up close: "We were not afraid, but there were times when we were plenty scared, and we were always impressed."

There you have it, a shelf of absorbing reading on all things bear. Whether you take on the whole list, pick and choose a few, or just find one that appeals to you, I'll be pleased, and I hope you also find your way to all the good ones I've left out. Titles deserving your attention keep coming to mind as I write this, especially those that accompanied *Grizzly Country* into print in those years when the modern bear-book boom was just beginning—Frank Dufresne's *No Room for Bears*, Walt Morey's *Gentle Ben*, Joe Van Wormer's *The World of the Black Bear*, and Ramona Morris and Desmond Morris's *Men and Pandas*—on and on the choices go.

For many of us, bears continue to be such amazing and compelling creatures that we just can't help ourselves; we have to read about them. And for those of us for whom reading isn't enough, eventually we have write about them.

And, as I have said before, in the half century and more since *Grizzly Country* appeared, this tremendous and warmly welcomed increase in the publication of bear books has continued, including many that are already clear candidates for classic status. Even my local bears in the Yellowstone region have been the subject of a generous assortment of excellent new bear books that vastly expand on Skinner's original book on the bears of that endlessly wondrous place. You'll find these new bear books much easier to identify and track down, and with any luck you'll soon be making your own list of favorites.

Happy reading.

Epilogue

A Word from the Bear

Route 7 north of Manchester, Vermont, skirts the Green Mountain National Forest for several miles, winding along the upper end of the Batten Kill Valley for about five miles. Then, not long after it passes through East Dorset, it crosses an unnoticed divide—your ears don't pop, or anything—and is in the valley of another smaller stream. There are forests in all directions, and in the summer the climate is best described as clammy.

It was 1982. I had been in Vermont going on five years, as executive director—a title of considerably more pomp than circumstance—of a wonderfully quirky little institution, the American Museum of Fly Fishing.

But five years was too long. I'd left work a little after six in the evening and driven north from my office, intending to go straight to my cottage in East Dorset, a village easily passed through without notice. The sullen, hazy weather was a perfect reflection of my mood.

I'd always wanted to live in New England, and the museum job was, I knew, a terrific experience that I would never forget, much less regret. But I was tired of everything eastern. I was frustrated with the impossibility of doing any of the several parts of the job as well as I would have liked; there was simply too much to do. I had started out as a historian-director-curator but gradually became a fundraiser, responsible for a series of banquets around the country and a growing amount of public relations work. It's not that I thought I was too good for that kind of work, but I didn't like it.

I was, I reminded myself impatiently, a historian, after all. I may not have been an especially productive historian, but I was a lot better at being a historian than at being a salesman.

Worse, I wanted to be somewhere else. I had tried New England and was ready to go back out West. I missed naïve, unfished trout that I could catch at will. I missed dry air. I missed young, sharp mountains that cast pointed shadows across sagebrush flats. I missed bears.

None of this was a surprise to me. I'd known all along, even the day I left Yellowstone and headed for Vermont to take the job, that I would eventually move back to the West. I don't think I realized how much the missing would ache, though. There were days when the car didn't seem to want to stop at my office in Manchester in the morning, when it yearned to go south an hour or so and swing onto the westbound lanes of Interstate 90. From there it would be simple: 2,500 miles and turn left at Livingston.

And there was nothing really stopping me. I'd already decided to leave soon, to let the museum's officers know, thank them for everything—a generous, irreplaceable everything—and drive away. Fast.

In five years I'd put out half a dozen books, all but one about the West, which was always on my mind. Some of my friends, both eastern and western, told me that I never gave Vermont a fair chance, that I was too busy writing and dreaming about the West, that the books about bears and canyons and cutthroat trout were just my way of refusing to wholly move to Vermont.

They were probably right. Vermont is a gorgeous place, with an engaging human and natural history. I loved my friends there. Also, here I was, in the heart of some of the best black bear country in North America; but I spent my time writing about grizzly bears. The local bears just weren't cooperative. I never saw them, not at all, in my considerable odd-hour wanderings along the streams and back roads.

So there I was driving along, silently whining and fuming over all these things—an especially frustrating day at the office, the West off there somewhere beckoning to me, a breathtakingly beautiful New England valley rolling past and me unable to take it to my heart, and my usual disappointment with myself that, once again, I was too restless to settle into a truly enviable place and live and work there.

Just before I reached East Dorset, before even its little steeples showed themselves above the trees, I decided not to go straight home. I'd drive on north a few more miles and stop in to visit a woman friend whom I could count on for pity and beer. This kind of self-indulgent funk was best savored when shared.

Oozing along the highway on the north edge of East Dorset, just past the parking lot of the Congregational Church, was a little swamp (God, I hope it's still there and not inhumed under some quaint shopping mall), home to the occasional great blue heron, Virginia rail, and the noisiest frogs I'd ever encountered. The road passed between it and the almost immediate slopes to its west. As I hurried through the one intersection, the roof of my cottage briefly visible up the hill, I could see the swamp along the right side of the road.

I was no more than a couple of hundred yards past the general store at the village junction when I noticed a commotion ahead on my right, in the shrubby trees down between the swamp and the road. Something was in there, and moving fast. A black form climbed from the thick tangle of saplings, up the short bank toward the road. I perked up from my daze of self-pity and discontent.

My eyes, never very trustworthy in a hurry, ventured an opinion: "A bear?"

My mind, after five years of bearlessness and in no mood for a joke, was not interested: "A dog, stupid."

My eyes got excited almost immediately. "It's a bear!"

My mind resisted, but was getting excited. "This is Vermont. I never see the bears. It's a dog."

Only a second had passed now since I saw it, and my eyes were furiously relaying solid, daylight-illuminated data to my mind. The decision was made: in unison, my eyes, my mind, and my mouth agreed. "Son of a bitch! It's a bear! *It's a bear.*" There was nothing in my mind now but amazed, grateful recognition, something like I would expect to feel if I saw an old friend I had been told was dead.

It was a bear, not big but perfect, soaked and shining from a dunk in the sluggish channel that drained the swamp and had previously yielded to my sight only a few dark brook trout. It was a bear, a lanky black bear now rolling along, up onto the road and across, heading west with that shambling, flat-footed, yardage-eating gait that always carries them out of sight before you're ready to let them go. There he was, there he went, and there I was—just now, just as I felt the way I did about everything—and it all fit.

I heard what he said. Oh, he didn't turn his head or anything, and no one else if they had been there would have heard anything, but I heard it. Just as he crossed the road in front of my approaching car, just as he could be sure I recognized him and knew what sent him and why, I heard the message: "Go."

He was into the woods and headed up the hill by the time I stopped the car just short of where he'd crossed the road. I hurried to the spot. His paws left shallow dents in the gravel of the berm, and a trail of paw-slapped water curved across the pavement toward the woods. My head was still buzzing with my own shout of recognition as I bent over the nearest print. After a moment I slowly put my hand down and spread it over the print, then rose and reached with the same hand out toward where the bear had disappeared into the trees.

ACKNOWLEDGMENTS AND SOURCE NOTES

My thanks go always first to my spouse, Marsha Karle, whose interest, patience, and encouragement keep me going. I can hardly begin to thank by name the many friends, colleagues, and known or anonymous reviewers whose suggestions and advice improved many of these selections in their earlier published forms. But I can single out my friend and former Yellowstone colleague Sue Consolo-Murphy—an expert's expert on science and resource management in Greater Yellowstone—whose thoughtful and professionally informed reading of the current manuscript improved it in many ways. Remaining errors are my own.

For the past twenty years or so, a goodly number of my books and I have been following editor Clark Whitehorn around from publisher to publisher because I trust his judgment on all sorts of publishing matters, because he always does such good work, and because he never fails to pay for lunch. By my count, this is at least the eighth of my books—either in a first or a revised edition—that we have worked on together, and thanks to him it is significantly improved from the first version of the manuscript that I submitted. Thanks again, Clark.

Most of what I've written about bears during the past forty years has been indebted in a general but essential way to the work of the International Association for Bear Research and Management. Through their always fascinating scientific journal and newsletter, and through their excellent series of conference proceedings, they have provided bear managers and the public with encyclopedically thorough reference materials on the bears of the world. I wish you would seriously consider joining and supporting them. For more information, just go to bearbiology.org.

This book is dedicated to two Canadian friends, Linda Wiggins and Steve Herrero, passionate citizens of the natural world whose work and views have been an inspiration to me and my wife Marsha for many years, and whose friendship we treasure.

All but one of the previously published chapters in this book have been substantially revised or even rewritten. The preface and chapters 6, 7, 12, 18, 19, 20, 21, and 22 are newly written for this book. What follows is both the publishing history of, and additional commentary on, the previously published chapters, with a few notes on sources for the others. References that are already included in my bibliography will be displayed in short citation form (author, title, page numbers), unless additional publishing information is needed.

Preface

The quotation of myself is from *The Fishing Life* (New York: Skyhorse, 2013), xiii.

1. Early Bears

When I started putting this book together, I was pretty sure that the first few paragraphs of this chapter had appeared in an essay I once wrote for a magazine, but now that I check my files I can't find any evidence of such a publication, so apparently they first appeared in the chapter "Nellie's Dream" in my book *Pregnant Bears and Crawdad Eyes*, 62–63. The rest is newly written for this book. Joyce Harvey's fine article in the *Lancaster Eagle-Gazette* about Andy the Bear is cited in full in the text, but here I thank her again.

2. The Bear Doesn't Know

This chapter originally appeared in my book *Mountain Time*, which is currently in print from the University of New Mexico Press, whose permission to reprint it is hereby acknowledged. I have revised and updated this chapter extensively for its appearance in the present book.

The quotation from Joseph Skutch is from *The Minds of Birds* (College Station: Texas A&M University Press, 1996), xiv.

The quotation from Steve Herrero is from "Conflicts between Man and Grizzly Bears in the National Parks of North America," 140.

The quotation from the first edition of my book *The Bears of Yellowstone* is from *The Bears of Yellowstone*, 147.

The quotation from Andy Russell is from *Grizzly Country*, 16.

I somehow feel I would be remiss were I not to list more of Yellowstone's own shelf of more recent bear books and monographs, in addition to the ones that I have already mentioned in the text. So here they are, all published after the cutoff date I have used in selecting the books that I consider in part 4 of this book.

I do recognize the arbitrary and otherwise flawed nature of such a list; that is, of distinguishing between books and a variety of other publications. For one thing, almost all of the most important scientific publications on bears in the past half century have been shorter works that appeared in a great variety of scientific journals and conference proceedings of one sort or another. But for most general readers, books in the broadest sense—that is, individual publications with their own covers—have always been the way to start to learn, and Yellowstone bears have been the subject of quite a few vitally important books and other separate publications, including a number of invaluable monographs and government reports.

I have to say that I offer this list with a sense of almost giddy wonder at its spectacular informational and literary richness. When I began work as a Yellowstone ranger-naturalist half a century ago, the only adult Yellowstone bear book was Milton Skinner's long-outdated and hard-to-find *Bears in the Yellowstone*, published almost fifty years earlier. When it came to authoritative scientific books about other park wildlife, except for Adolph Murie's pathbreaking *Ecology of the Coyote in the Yellowstone*—itself more than thirty years old—and Mary Meagher's soon-to-be-published and still essential *The Bison of Yellowstone National Park*, we rangers were interpreting the park's many wonders from the thinnest of easily accessible sources. Today, I'm thrilled to say, there's so much to read that it's almost impossible to keep up.

I will restrict this list to books that are entirely or in good part about the bears of greater Yellowstone, that being a geographical area whose controversial and gradually expanded boundaries many of these studies were important in helping to define and even celebrate. In order of publication date, they are: John Craighead and Frank Craighead, *Grizzly Bear Prehibernation and Denning Activities as Determined by Radiotracking* (Washington DC: Wildlife Society, Wildlife Monograph 32, 1972); Committee on Appropriations, United States Senate, Fifty-Fourth Congress, Second Session, Special Hearing, *Proposed Critical Habitat Area for Grizzly Bears* (Washington DC: U.S. Government Printing Office, 1977); John Craighead, *A Proposed Delineation of Critical Grizzly Bear Habitat in the Yellowstone Region* (n.p.: The Bear Biology Association, 1980); Bill Schneider, *Where the Grizzly Walks* (Missoula MT: Mountain, 1977); Frank Craighead, *Track of the Grizzly* (San Francisco: Sierra Club Books, 1979); John Craighead, J. S. Sumner, and G. B. Scaggs, *A Definitive System for Analysis of Grizzly Bear Habitat and Other Wilderness Resources: Utilizing LANDSAT Multispectral Imagery and Computer Technology* (Missoula: University of Montana Foundation and Wildlife-Wildlands Institute, 1982); Thomas McNamee, *The Grizzly Bear* (New York: Alfred Knopf, 1984); Doug Peacock, *Grizzly Years: In Search of the American Wilderness* (New York: Henry Holt, 1990); John Craighead, Jay Sumner, and John Alexander Mitchell, *The Grizzly Bears of Yellowstone: Their Ecology in the Yellowstone Ecosystem* (Covelo CA: Island, 1995); Mark S. Boyce, Bonnie M. Blanchard, Richard R. Knight, and Christopher Servheen, *Population Viability for Grizzly Bears: A Critical Review* (n.p.: International Association for Bear Research and Management Monograph Series Number 4, 2001); Jim Cole, *Lives of Grizzlies: Montana and Wyoming* (Helena MT: Farcountry Press, 2004); Alice Wondrak Biel, *Do (Not) Feed the Bears: The Fitful History of Wildlife and Tourists in Yel-*

lowstone (Lawrence: University Press of Kansas, 2006); Bob Murphy, *Bears I Have Known* (Helena MT: Riverbend, 2006); C. C. Schwartz, M. A. Haroldson, G. C. White, R. B. Harris, S. Cherry, K. A. Keating, D. Moody, and C. Servheen, *Temporal, Spatial, and Environmental Influences on the Demographics of Grizzly Bears in the Greater Yellowstone Ecosystem* (Washington DC: Wildlife Monographs 161, 2006); James Halfpenny, *Yellowstone Bears in the Wild*; Doug Peacock and Andrea Peacock, *In the Presence of Grizzlies: The Ancient Bond Between Men and Bears* (Guilford CT: Lyons, 2009); Jim Cole, *Blindsided: Surviving a Grizzly Attack and Still Loving the Great Bear* (New York: St. Martin's Press, 2010); Michael Leach, *Grizzlies On My Mind: Essays of Adventure, Love, and Heartache from Yellowstone Country* (Portland OR: Westwind, 2014); Kathleen Snow, *Taken by Bear in Yellowstone: More than a Century of Harrowing Encounters Between Grizzlies and Humans* (New York: Lyons, 2016); Jerry Mernin, *Yellowstone Ranger: Stories from a Life in Yellowstone* (Helena MT: Riverbend, 2016); P. J. White, Kerry Gunther, and Frank T. van Manen, eds., *Yellowstone Grizzly Bears: Ecology and Conservation of an Icon of Wildness* (Yellowstone National Park: Yellowstone Forever and the U.S. Geological Survey, 2017); Cat Urbigkit, *Return of the Grizzly: Sharing the Range with Yellowstone's Top Predator* (New York: Skyhorse, 2019); and Barrie Gilbert, *One of Us: A Biologist's Walk Among Bears* (Victoria BC: Friesens, 2019). I apologize to authors I may inadvertently have missed; I mean well.

Were I compelled at gunpoint to suggest where to start with Yellowstone bear books, especially which ones to have for a core reference set, I would suggest three that have been mentioned earlier: P. J. White, Kerry Gunther, and Frank T. van Manen, eds., *Yellowstone Grizzly Bears: Ecology and Conservation of an Icon of Wildness*; Jim Halfpenny's *Yellowstone Bears in the Wild*: and Alice Wondrak Biel's *Do (Not) Feed the Bears*. Those three will give you an enviably thorough historical and scientific context for enjoying Yellowstone bear country and becoming informed on the various issues and crises that face the bears and the wild country they inhabit there.

Last and far from least, for a comprehensive and uniquely instructive overview of the long, complicated history of bear-caused human fatalities in and near Yellowstone National Park, I direct you to Lee Whittlesey's penetrating and exhaustively researched *Death in Yellowstone: Accidents and Foolhardiness in the First National Park*, 2nd ed. (Lanham MD: Roberts Rinehart, 2014). Make sure you get this edition and not the previous ones, as it contains the fullest account of early park bear attacks ever compiled. Lee is an outstanding and tenacious researcher. The bear-attack section of his book is by itself a significant and important scholarly contribution to our understanding of bears and humans in Greater Yellowstone.

3. Arts and Craps

A shorter version of this story first appeared as a chapter in an anthology, *Mark of the Bear: Legend and Lore of an American Icon* (San Francisco: Sierra Club Books/Tehabi, 1996), 30–33, which I edited. Though my stated purpose in the present book is to include only material that didn't appear in any of my previous bear books, I have made an exception here. *Mark of the Bear* was a coffee-table book, and because such books go notoriously unread, and especially so when the photographs are as fine as they were in this one, I have chosen to include it in a much-revised form here.

Seton's story of the tricky grizzly appeared in his *Biography of a Grizzly*, 136–40. The quote of Charles Preston appeared in "The Long and Winding Road: Yellowstone Grizzly Bears since *The Biography of a Grizzly*," his thoughtful afterword to a new edition of the *Biography* (Norman: University of Oklahoma Press, 2015), 207.

For excellent interpretive discussions of "bear trees," and other bear sign—much more detailed than I offer in this chapter—besides the wonderful new book by Benjamin Kilham that I mention and quote in the text, see James Halfpenny, *Yellowstone Bears in the Wild*, 51–61; and Stephen Herrero, *Bear Attacks*, 3rd ed., 184–97. For a delightful quantity of engaging historical (pre-1930) anecdotal material and opinion about bear trails, tracks, tree marking behavior, and other sign, I can't recommend too highly Ernest

Thompson Seton's *Bears, Coons, Badgers, Skunks, and Weasels*, vol. 2, pt. 1 of *Lives of Game Animals*, where discussions of these matters as they involve both grizzly bears and black bears appear on pages 42–44, 97–98, 136–40.

The quotations from the Kilham book, *Out on a Limb*, are both from page 56.

The quotation from Kurtén's *The Cave Bear Story* on the *Bärenschliffe* phenomenon is from page 98.

4. Nervous Neighbors

Apparently this originally appeared in my book *Pregnant Bears and Crawdad Eyes*, 82–90. I could have sworn it also appeared in article form somewhere, but I guess not. It has been updated and revised for its appearance here.

The Steve Herrero quotes are from the most recent edition of his milestone book, *Bear Attacks*, 3rd ed., 214 (about the black bear) and 215 (about the grizzly bear).

As the evolutionary story in this chapter seems to me the most interesting part, I invite you to consider any or all of the following discussions of bear evolution: Stephen Herrero, "Aspects of Evolution and Adaptation in American Black Bears (Ursus americanus Pallas) and Brown and Grizzly Bears (U. arctos Linné.) in North America," in *Bears—Their Biology and Management*, ed. Stephen Herrero, a selection of papers and discussion from the Second International Conference on Bear Research and Management (Morges, Switzerland, International Union for Conservation of Nature and Natural Resources, 1974), 221–31; Bjorn Kurtén, *The Cave Bear Story*; Stephen Herrero, *Bear Attacks*, 3rd ed.; Bruce McLellan and David C. Reiner, "A Review of Bear Evolution," *International Conference on Bear Research and Management* 9, no. 1 (1994): 85–96; and Charles C. Schwartz, S. D. Miller, and Mark A. Haroldson, "Grizzly Bear," in *Wild Mammals of North America: Biology, Management, and Conservation*, ed. G. A. Feldhamer, B. C. Thompson, and J. A. Chapman, 556–57 (Baltimore MD: John Hopkins University Press, 2003).

But, all of those excellent scientific sources having been read, I should introduce one of those delightful twists of interpretation that have so long characterized our increasing understanding of wildlife populations: a recent paper by David J. Mattson, Stephen Herrero, and Troy Merrill, "Are Black Bears a Factor in the Restoration of North American Grizzly Bear Populations?" *Ursus* 16, no. 1 (2005): 11–30. These authors propose that in certain habitats, especially where the available foods are those preferred by both species (i.e., nearly complete dietary overlap), black bears may compete with grizzly bears so successfully that black bears may be a primary factor in limiting grizzly bear numbers or preventing grizzly bear populations from becoming established. Thus, though grizzly bears are overwhelmingly favored in direct confrontations between individuals of the two species, on a population level black bears may sometimes "win" the competition for space. This, the authors say, is most likely to happen in places where the black bears are already well established and the grizzly bears were either late comers, as in most of the eastern U.S. historically, or where grizzly bears were eliminated during the past two centuries but black bears endured, as in areas where attempts might be made to reestablish grizzly bear populations in the American West.

5. Almost My Favorite Bear Story

The story I quote originally appeared in Lewis R. Freeman, *Down the Yellowstone* (New York: Dodd, Mead, 1922), 37–43. It seems even more odd to me that I should have forgotten to include this story in *Yellowstone Bear Tales* when I did put it in a non-bear book, *Yellowstone's Ski Pioneers: Peril and Heroism on the Winter Trail* (Worland WY: High Plains, 1991).

8. Embryonic Journeys

This piece originally appeared in much shorter form as "Stopping Nature's Clock," in *Backpacker* magazine, October 1989, then in revised form, retitled "Embryonic Journeys" in my book *Pregnant Bears and Crawdad Eyes*, 24–30. It has been further revised and updated here.

The early quote about no bears ever being found pregnant is from John Brickell, *The Natural History of North Carolina* (Dublin: self-pub., 1743), 112.

The quote from Terry DeBruyn about the timing of blastocyst implantation is from his book *Walking with Bears*, 15.

Jeremy Schmidt's quote is from his book *Lehman Caves* (Great Basin National Park NV: Great Basin Natural History Association, 1987), 4.

For a review of embryonic diapause, see Rodney A. Mead, "Embryonic Diapause in Vertebrates," *Journal of Experimental Zoology* 266 (1993): 629–41. For a review of the biology of bear hibernation, see Ralph A. Nelson, G. Edgar Folk Jr., Egbert W. Pfeiffer, John J. Craighead, Charles C. Jonkel, and Dianne L. Steiger, "Behavior, Biochemistry, and Hibernation in Black, Grizzly, and Polar Bears," *International Conference on Bear Research and Management* 5 (1983): 284–90. For a thorough popular review of hibernation and, for that matter, pretty much everything else about the natural history of Yellowstone bears, see, again, James Halfpenny, *Yellowstone Bears in the Wild*.

9. Ferocious Beasts

This first appeared with the same title in the late lamented magazine *Country Journal* (April 1988): 72–74, and then in expanded form, retitled "Taming the Giant Weasels," in my book *Pregnant Bears and Crawdad Eyes*, 127–31. It has been further revised and expanded for its appearance here.

The quotation from Shepard and Sanders appeared in *The Sacred Paw*, xii.

The Keith Thomas quotation is from his book *Man and the Natural World* (New York: Pantheon Press, 1982), 41.

10. Bear Attacks

This originally appeared in shorter form as the foreword to a new revised edition of Stephen Herrero's classic work on the subject, *Bear Attacks: Their Causes and Avoidance.*

The quotation from Steve Herrero is from "Conflicts between Man and Grizzly Bears in the National Parks of North America," 140.

11. The Question Answered

This is a revised, expanded, but still brief excerpt from a book I wrote, and that my spouse, Marsha Karle, illustrated with dozens of lovely watercolors: *This High Wild Country: A Celebration of Waterton-Glacier International Peace Park* (Albuquerque: University of New Mexico Press, 2010), 89.

12. On Skipping *The Revenant*

The John Myers quote appears in his book, *The Saga of Hugh Glass*, 3.

Chapters 13–17

The material gathered into the five chapters of part 3 of this book are all taken, with considerable rewriting, from my book *Real Alaska: Finding Our Way in the Wild Country* (Mechanicsburg PA: Stackpole, 2001). Selections from that book used here are mightily adapted to the point that it serves no purpose to try to list page numbers for them. I am extremely grateful to my friend, Stackpole publisher Judith Schnell, for permission to reprint such an extended portion of that book here.

The "Readings and Sources" section of *Real Alaska* provides a reasonably extensive listing of books and other publications relating to the issues and places explored in the book. Here I list two of the sources specifically mentioned in the present material: Thomas Mangelsen, *Images of Nature: The Photographs of Thomas D. Mangelsen* (Fairfield CT: Hugh Lauter Levin 1989) and Robert Griggs, "Our Greatest National Monument," *National Geographic* 30, no. 3 (1921): 219–92.

My happy little recollection of time spent at Katmai is not intended to reassure readers that things are all hunky-dory there. Like bear management in many places, management of the Katmai National Park and Preserve bears continues to be controversial, and I hope you will pay attention. There are several books relating all or in good part to the bears of Katmai National Park: Tamara Olson and Ronald Squibb, *Brown Bears of Brooks River* (Kodiak AK: Squibb, 1993); Katherine Ringsmuth, *At the Heart of Katmai: An Administrative History of the Brooks River Area, with Special Emphasis on Bear Management in Katmai National Park and Preserve, 1912–2006* (Washington DC: National Park Service, 2013); Sherry Simpson, *Dominion of Bears: Living with Wildlife in Alaska* (Lawrence: University Press of Kansas, 2013); Barrie Gilbert, *One of Us: A Biologist's Walk Among Bears* (Victoria BC: Friesens, 2019); and Michael Fitz, *The Bears of Brooks Falls: Wildlife and Survival on Alaska's Brooks River* (Woodstock VT: Countryman, 2021). As I've often said in this book, the books are only the beginning; there's a huge quantity of science and journalism to be found easily in shorter publications as well.

Epilogue

This little recollection appeared in very nearly this same form in my book *Pregnant Bears and Crawdad Eyes*, 170–73.

BIBLIOGRAPHY

Today's collectors, bibliographers, and readers of bear books might well invoke King Solomon's cautionary advice in Ecclesiastes 12:12 that, "of making many books there is no end; and much study is a weariness of the flesh." Even so, I do hope that someday soon some energetic student of bear literature will publish a nice, hefty bibliography of bear books. It would be a grand book of many parts—a reader's treasure chest of wonderful opportunities. My ambition in the following list is by comparison severely modest. I list here only titles that I mentioned in the text of this book and offer it only as convenience to readers wishing to pursue some point or topic I've made (additional titles, not mentioned in the text, are listed in the Sources). Many of the books listed here have sizeable bibliographies of their own that will serve you well on your own searches. Some of the following books have gone through numerous editions. Unless otherwise noted, I list only the first edition of each here; an online search will fill in the rest of their bibliographical sagas and, in most cases, will alert you to the availability of new, used, or digital copies you can acquire for your very own.

Beatty, Matthew. *Bears of Yosemite*. Yosemite National Park: Yosemite Natural History Association, 1946.

Bonner, T. D. *The Life and Adventures of James P. Beckwourth: Mountaineer, Scout, and Pioneer, and Chief of the Crow Nation of Indians*. London: Sampson Low, Son, 1856.

Brown, David. *The Grizzly in the Southwest: Documentary of an Extinction*. Norman: University of Oklahoma Press, 1985.

Brown, Gary. *The Great Bear Almanac* New York: Lyons, 1993.

Claar, James, and Paul Schullery, eds. *Bears—Their Biology and Management*. Yellowstone National Park and Missoula MT: International Association for Bear Research and Management and the Yellowstone Center for Resources, 1994. A selection of papers from the Ninth International Conference on Bear Research and Management, Missoula MT, February 23–28, 1992.

Croke, Vicki. *The Lady and the Panda: The True Adventures of the First American Explorer to Bring Back China's Most Exotic Animal*. New York: Random House, 2005.

DeBruyn, Terry. *Walking with Bears*. New York: Lyons, 1999.

Dillon, Richard. *The Legend of Grizzly Adams: California's Greatest Mountain Man.* New York: Coward, McCann and Geophagan, 1966.

Dufresne, Frank. *No Room for Bears*. New York: Holt, Rinehart and Winston, 1965.

Erickson, Albert, John Nellor, and George Petrides. *The Black Bear in Michigan*. Ann Arbor: Michigan State University Agricultural Experiment Station, Research Bulletin 4, 1964.

Faulkner, William. *Go Down, Moses*. New York: Random House, 1942.

Gowans, Fred R., *Mountain Man and Grizzly*. Orem UT: Mountain Grizzly, 1986.

Halfpenny, James. *Yellowstone Bears in the Wild*. Helena MT: Riverbend, 2007.

Hallowell, Alfred Irving. "Bear Ceremonialism in the Northern Hemisphere." *American Anthropologist* 28 (January–March 1926): 2–175.

Harkness, Ruth. *The Baby Giant Panda*. New York: Carrick and Evans, 1938.

——. *The Lady and the Panda: An Adventure*. New York: Carrick and Evans, 1938.

Haynes, Bessie, and Edgar Haynes. *The Grizzly Bear: Portraits from Life*. Norman: University of Oklahoma Press, 1966.

Herrero, Steve. *Bear Attacks: Their Causes and Avoidance*. 3rd ed. Guildford CT: Globe Pequot/Lyons, 2018.

——. "Conflicts between Man and Grizzly Bears in the National Parks of North America." In *Bears—Their Biology and Management*. A selection of papers from the Third International Conference on Bear Research and Management, June 1974, edited by Michael R. Pelton, Jack W. Lentfer, and G. Edgar Folks. Morges, Switzerland: International Union for the Conservation of Nature and Natural Resources, 1976.

Hittell, Theodore. *The Adventures of James Capen Adams, Mountaineer and Grizzly Bear Hunter of California*. San Francisco: Towne and Bacon, 1860; rpt. New York: Charles Scribner's Sons, 1911.

Holzworth, John. *The Twin Grizzlies of Admiralty Island*. Philadelphia: J. B. Lippincott, 1932.

——. *The Wild Grizzlies of Alaska*. New York: G. P. Putnam's Sons, 1930.

Howe, John R. Howe. *Bear Man of Admiralty Island: A Biography of Allen E. Hasselborg*. Fairbanks: University of Alaska Press, 1996.

Irving, Washington. *The Adventures of Captain Bonneville, USA*. New York: G. P. Putnam's Sons, 1898.

Kilham, Benjamin. *Out on a Limb: What Black Bears Taught Me about Intelligence and Intuition.* White River Junction VT: Chelsea Green, 2013.

Kurtén, Björn. *The Cave Bear Story: Life and Death of a Vanished Animal.* New York: Columbia University Press, 1976.

Lapham, Heather A., and Gregory A. Waselkov, eds. *Bears: Archeological and Ethnohistorical Perspectives in Native Eastern North America.* Gainesville: University of Florida Press, 2020.

Major, Charles. *The Bears of Blue River.* Philadelphia: Curtis, 1901.

McCracken, Howard. *Alaska Bear Trails.* Garden City NY: Doubleday, Doran, 1931.

———. *The Beast That Walks Like Man: The Lore, Legend and History of the Grizzly Bear.* New York: Hanover House, 1955.

———. *The Biggest Bear on Earth.* Philadelphia: Stokes, 1943.

———. *The Flaming Bear.* Philadelphia: J. B. Lippincott, 1951.

McMillion, Scott. *Mark of the Grizzly.* Helena MT: Falcon, 1998.

Merriam, C. Hart. *The Mammals of the Adirondack Region.* New York: L. S. Foster, 1884.

———. *Review of the grizzly and big brown Bears of North America (genus Ursus) with description of a new genus, Vetularctos.* Washington DC: Government Printing Office. U.S. Department of Agriculture, Bureau of Biological Survey, North American Fauna No. 41, February 9, 1918.

Miller, Joaquin. *True Bear Stories.* Chicago: Rand, McNally, 1900.

Milne, A. A. *Winnie-the-Pooh.* London: Methuen, 1926.

Mills, Enos. *The Grizzly: Our Greatest Wild Animal.* Boston: Houghton Mifflin, 1919.

Morey, Walt. *Gentle Ben.* New York: E. P. Dutton, 1965.

Morris, Ramona, and Desmond Morris. *Men and Pandas.* New York: McGraw-Hill, 1966.

Mullins, Linda. *The Teddy Bear Men: Theodore Roosevelt and Clifford Berryman.* Cumberland MD: Hobby House, 1987.

Murie, Olaus. *A Field Guide to Animal Tracks.* Boston: Houghton Mifflin, 1954.

Myers, John Myers. *The House at Pooh Corner.* London: Methuen, 1928.

———. *The Saga of Hugh Glass: Pirate, Pawnee, and Mountain Man.* New York: Little, Brown, 1963.

Pickett, William D. "Memories of a Bear Hunter." In *Hunting At High Altitudes,* edited by George Bird Grinnell, 11–294. New York: Harper & Brothers, 1913.

Punke, Michael. *The Revenant: A Novel of Revenge.* New York: Carol and Graf, 2002.

Reid, Thomas Mayne. *The Boy Hunters.* Boston: Charles E. Brown, 1853.

———. *Bruin: The Grand Bear Hunt.* Boston: Ticknor and Fields, 1860.

Rockwell, David. *Giving Voice to Bear: North American Indian Myths, Rituals, and Images of the Bear.* Rev. ed. Boulder CO: Roberts Rinehart, 2002.

Roosevelt, Theodore, Jr., and Kermit Roosevelt. *Trailing the Giant Panda.* New York: Scribner's, 1929.

Russell, Andy, ed. *Great Bear Adventures: True Tales from the Wild.* Toronto: Key Porter, 1987.

———. *Grizzly Country.* New York: Alfred Knopf, 1967.

Schaller, George B., Hu Jinchu, Pen Wensi, and Zhu Jing. *The Giant Pandas of Wolong*. Chicago: University of Chicago Press, 1985.

———. *The Last Panda*. Chicago: University of Chicago Press, 1993.

Schullery, Paul, ed. *American Bears: Selections from the Writings of Theodore Roosevelt*. Boulder CO: Colorado Associated University Press and the Outdoor Life Book Club, 1983.

———. *The Bear Hunter's Century: Profiles from the Golden Age of Bear Hunting*. New York: Dodd, Mead, 1988.

———. *The Bears of Yellowstone*. Yellowstone National Park: Yellowstone Library and Museum Association, 1980.

———. Introduction to *The Beast that Walks Like Man: The Story of the Grizzly Bear*, by Harold McCracken. Lanham MD: Roberts Rinehart, 2003. First published 1955 by Hanover House (New York).

———. *Lewis and Clark Among the Grizzlies: Legend and Legacy in the American West*. Guilford CT: Falcon, 2002.

———. *Mountain Time*. New York: Nick Lyons/Schocken, 1984.

———. *Pregnant Bears and Crawdad Eyes: Excursions and Encounters in Animal Worlds*. Seattle: The Mountaineers, 1991.

———, ed. *Yellowstone Bear Tales: Adventures, Mishaps, and Discoveries among the World's Most Famous Bears*. Boulder CO: Roberts Rinehart, 1991.

———. "Yogi Lives: The Evolving Image of the Bears of Yellowstone." In *Greater Yellowstone Predators: Ecology and Conservation in a Changing Landscape*. Proceedings of the Third Biennial Scientific Conference on the Greater Yellowstone Ecosystem, September 24–27, 1995. Edited by A. P. Curlee, A. Gillesberg, and D. Casey, 3–11. Yellowstone National Park WY: Northern Rockies Conservation Cooperative and National Park Service, Jackson WY, and Yellowstone National Park.

Seton, Ernest Seton. *Bears, Coons, Badgers, Skunks, and Weasels*. Vol. 2, pt. 1 of *Lives of Game Animals*. Garden City NY: Doubleday, Doran, 1929.

———. *The Biography of a Grizzly*. New York: Grosset and Dunlap, 1900.

———. *Life Histories of Northern Animals: An Account of the Mammals of Manitoba*. New York: Charles Scribner's Sons, 1909.

———. *Monarch the Big Bear of Tallac*. New York: Charles Scribner's Sons, 1904.

———. *Wahb: The Biography of a Grizzly*. Norman: University of Oklahoma Press, 2015.

Shepard, Paul, and Barry Sanders. *The Sacred Paw: The Bear in Nature, Myth, and Literature*. New York: Viking, 1985.

Shields, George Oliver. *Hunting in the Great West*. 5th ed. Chicago: Donohue, Henneberry, 1890.

Shoemaker, Henry. *The Black Bear of Pennsylvania*. Altoona PA: Times Tribune, 1921.

Skinner, Milton. *Bears in the Yellowstone*. Chicago: A. C. McClurg, 1925.

Snyder, Susan. *Bear in Mind: The California Grizzly*. Berkeley CA: Heyday, 2003.

Spencer, Howard. *The Black Bear and Its Status in Maine*. Augusta: State of Maine Department of Inland Fisheries and Game, 1961.

Stevens, Montague. *Meet Mr. Grizzly: A Saga on the Passing of the Grizzly Bear*. Albuquerque: University of New Mexico Press, 1943.

Storer, Tracy, and Lloyd Tevis. *California Grizzly*. Berkeley: University of California Press, 1955.

Underwood, William Lyman. *Wild Brother: Strangest of True Stories from the North Woods*. Boston: Atlantic Monthly, 1921.

Utley, Francis, Lynn Bloom, and Arthur Kinney, eds. 2nd ed. *Bear, Man, and God: Eight Approaches to William Faulkner's "The Bear."* New York: Random House, 1971.

Van Tramp, John C. *Prairie and Rocky Mountain Adventures*. St. Louis: J. H. Miller, 1859.

Van Wormer, Joe. *The World of the Black Bear*. Philadelphia: Lippincott, 1966.

Verne, Jules. *The Fur Country*. New York: Wm. L. Allison, 1874.

White, P. J., Kerry Gunther, and Frank T. van Manen, eds. *Yellowstone Grizzly Bears: Ecology and Conservation of an Icon of Wildness*. Yellowstone National Park WY: Yellowstone Forever and the U.S. Geological Survey, 2017.

Wright, William. *Ben, the Black Bear*. New York: Charles Scribner's Sons, 1910.

——. *The Grizzly Bear: The Narrative of a Hunter-Naturalist*. New York: Charles Scribner's Sons, 1909.